LIGHT OF A STAR

To Paul and 'Potsy'

LIGHT OF A STAR

Gwen Robyns

LESLIE FREWIN : LONDON

First published 1968 by Leslie Frewin Publishers Limited,
15 Hay's Mews, Berkeley Square, London W1

This book is set in Fournier
Printed by Anchor Press and
Bound by William Brendon,
both of Tiptree, Essex

Contents

Introduction

'THE TRUE STORY of Vivien Leigh cannot be told for a hundred years,' Elizabeth Frank said as we discussed her friendship with the actress.

But I disagree. The further I became involved in the research of this book the more I realised that the story must be told now before people's minds become dim and the edges of their anecdotes blurred.

There was also a feeling among the tight-lipped, loyal trustees that only a person who knew Vivien Leigh intimately should have the honour of translating her image into print.

Again I disagree. How much better to have no preconceived ideas about the lady, no prejudices, no blind spots, but to let the story be told through the people who knew her intimately and made up her world. This is what I have done.

When I undertook to write this book, reluctantly I must admit, I thought it was a straightforward story of a pretty girl who by sheer work and application became a competent, world-known actress and gathered a title on the way up.

Only when I began to delve did I find that like the iceberg one-seventh was above water for all to behold. But it was the dark, mysterious, submerged rest that gave a clue to the real substance of her character.

There is another reason I feel that this story should be told now and not in ten, twenty or a hundred years' time. When I asked an intelligent young friend on an erudite

Sunday newspaper to check a fact in the library she answered:

'Oh Vivien Leigh. She was an actress, wasn't she?'

Such is the speed of forgetfulness in this undignified age. She must know about the courage, the sheer professionalism, the brilliance and beauty, the loyalty and the abundant loving and giving that made Vivien Leigh unique. She must know now.

I would like to thank Miss Leigh's friends – and you know who you are – who trusted me with confidences. Also Leslie Frewin whose idea the book was and the Fleet Street colleagues – Jack Hallam, Harry Treherne, Arthur Davis and Rowarth Lintott – for their realistic help on the days when I thought this book would never be written.

Hollycourt Farm   *July 1968*
Northleigh
Oxfordshire

Someone Luminous

THE GREATEST ATTRIBUTE any actress can have is star quality . . . star light. It is a brilliance that stretches across the footlights and has no boundaries. It is the authority to hold an audience spellbound.

It is even more. It is a personal magic that distinguishes one human being from ten million others.

This Vivien Leigh had as few actresses of this century.

When she walked into a room you were aware that here was someone different . . . someone apart . . . someone luminous. Her inner fire, gaiety and vitality were infectious and even from across the footlights you sensed the strength of her personality.

She had not only great beauty, and a brilliant intellect, but she balanced being a leading actress and a woman, without sacrificing herself.

Vivien Leigh was a strange, intriguing mixture – complex, loving, demanding, inspiring, totally enchanting . . . that is how her friends saw her.

As Tennessee Williams, as much poet as playwright, wrote of her in *Life* magazine: 'Vivien, above all else, is incomparably graceful. When she takes the stage she commands it as if she first arrived there suspended from the bill of a stork. She moves like a marvellous dancer, both on and off stage. All these wonderful gifts she has with no apparent regard for her personal vulnerability; in other words, she is not only a stunning actress but a lady with the most important part of that intricate composition, which is kindness of the heart.'

9

She had 'class', as the Americans say. Other English actresses today have that – Dame Edith Evans, Vanessa Redgrave, Margaret Leighton, Audrey Hepburn, Rachel Kempson, to name a few. But Vivien Leigh invested hers with star rating. She was born with a built-in distinction and natural glamour and was a tribute to her own high standard of perfectionism.

She was determined to – and did – make herself into the Vivien Leigh that the world adored.

Like Garbo and Dietrich, her beauty and glamour became a legend in her own lifetime but she herself was never impressed. She disliked intensely to be tagged a 'porcelain beauty'. She found the description vulgar and boring. She used her beauty merely as a working tool rather as Maria Callas cossets her vocal chords and Margot Fonteyn her ten toes.

Tennessee Williams described her individual beauty as 'delicately flamboyant as an orchid', others have likened her to an exotic Siamese cat. She had magnolia pale skin, wide-set luminous green eyes, a slowly upward-curving smile, delicate pert nose and a chin that whittled away to a point.

All women who are stars of real magnitude in their own lifetime have a physical magic that places them in a class of their own. Marilyn Monroe, Jean Harlow, Elizabeth Taylor, Rita Hayworth have flesh impact. They have three-dimensional flesh that photographs like flesh and from the twenty-third row of the stalls you can reach right out and touch it.

Garbo, Dietrich, Katherine Hepburn and Vivien Leigh have bones. They have bones so chiselled that every turn of the head produces a new set of facial planes and a fresh impact of their unique beauty.

For tall, statuesque beauties like Garbo, bone beauty comes easier. But for a jewel-size face like Vivien Leigh's, the challenge was so much greater. In the theatre especially she could have been swamped so easily. That she was not is a tribute to her own determination and dynamic personality.

In talking to writer Robert Ottaway about beauty, she said: 'In Britain, an attractive woman is somehow suspect. If there is talent as well it is overshadowed. Beauty and brains just can't be entertained; someone has been too extravagant. This does not happen in America and on the Continent, for the looks of a woman are considered a positive advertisement for her gifts and don't detract from them.'

In her personal life she could be wickedly crisp and almost brutal in her frankness. If an author asked her to read his play she would never say, 'Darling, it's wonderful but unfortunately I won't be free for ages.' She would read it and, if she thought so, just say, 'It's terrible.'

It is reported that in one of the shortest interviews of all time Hollywood columnist Hedda Hopper said, 'I suppose you are too busy to read the papers?'

'On the contrary,' said Vivien sweetly, 'I read all the papers except the one in which your column appears.'

'Aren't you afraid of her?' a friend who overheard the conversation asked.

'What? Me afraid of a hat?' Vivien snorted.

One soured recipient of her anger described her as 'a galvanised waxwork' and another 'as calculating as a slot machine'.

Vivien Leigh's strength lay in her immense resilience to the buffetings she took in life and her calculated use of that non-permissive four letter word. As the Victorian ladies swooned when it suited them, Vivien spat profanities. She became famous for them.

It was in subtle differences that you noticed the regal

respect this waif of a woman inspired among her fellow workers on the stage or film set. Technicians and cameramen, blasé of beauty, respected her good manners. They, in turn, became quieter, less boisterous when she was present. In the freemasonry of the acting profession, where everyone is on Christian name terms, Vivien Leigh permitted only those very close to her this liberty. To the rest, in the traditional manner, she was always 'Miss Leigh'.

She looked, felt and behaved as a star. She was completely dedicated to being professional and was never known to be late on the stage or set. She was there – ready – immaculately dressed and made up, word perfect and bathed in a cloud of fragrance.

She adored excitement. She would have loved to have been in the centre of a revolution or in the middle of a war or some terrific tragedy. If she had lived in another era, she would have probably gone to hottest Australia, darkest Africa or found part of the White Nile. She was quite fearless about people and things. She liked to do things that other people had not done, to go to places where other people had not been.

Her personal courage and humour were immense. A fortnight before Vivien died Mary Ure and her husband Robert Shaw dined, together with George Cukor, at her house. 'It was such an especially wonderful evening that next day I said to Robert I must send Vivien a great bouquet of flowers. And I did. I received a card back written by her and after thanking me she said, "I only thought you got this (tuberculosis) in undeveloped countries." '

One of her most endearing qualities was her generosity and personal involvement with people. There was nothing casual about her love and she cherished her friends dearly.

Wherever she was in the world and no matter how late she had got to bed, the first thing every morning she checked her personal diary. There she had written all the birthdays, anniversaries and special days – hundreds of them.

Gifts, flowers, telegrams and letters were then sent off like winged messengers all over the world. It was an immense and loving task that she never neglected.

Her gifts were exceptional and extraordinarily personal, and she went to endless trouble to arrange and package them. Whenever possible, she never sent cut flowers simply but had the florist arrange them in some enchanting piece of china she thought the person might like.

Actress Renee Asherson delights in the clear, beautiful green jug which was filled with sweet-smelling flowers and sent her by Vivien when her husband Robert Donat died. Two small vases are mementoes of the opening night of *A Streetcar Named Desire*. There is scarcely a well-known theatrical mantelshelf in England that does not boast a piece of porcelain from Vivien Leigh.

When times were stringent after the war and she had been in America, she struggled through the customs with armfuls of aerosols for her friends' bathrooms. Elizabeth Frank cherishes a birthday gift of *The Owl and the Pussycat* in French. 'No one but Vivien would have thought of that for me.'

Says Godfrey Winn, 'People who never met her except across the footlights did not realise how, in her private life, she had such compassion and interest in everyone.

'After I returned from Hong Kong I was ill with a virus and she rang me up reproachfully later to say, "Why didn't you let me know? I would have come to sit with you."

'Giving flowers to sick people is easy. Giving that precious commodity time is far more expensive for someone who had such a full life. But she always found time for everyone.'

She said of herself, 'Scorpions burn themselves out and eat themselves up and they are careless about themselves – like me.

'I swing between happiness and misery and I cry easily. I'm a mixture of my mother's determination and my father's optimism. I'm part prude and part non-conformist and I say what I think and I don't dissemble. I'm a mixture of French, Irish and Yorkshire, and perhaps that's what it all is.'

Education and Marriage

WITHIN DISTANCE OF Mount Everest and Kanchenjunga, Vivian Mary Hartley was born in a bungalow on a beautiful evening on 5th November 1913, in Darjeeling, India. Her mother had been married for two years to a young exchange broker, Ernest Hartley.

The war years that followed prevented the little family from returning to England until Vivian first came to school when she was six years old. But the love of mountains and the out-of-doors was to remain with her all her life.

The Convent of the Sacred Heart at Roehampton, a few miles outside London, was a natural choice for Mrs Hartley to select for her daughter. An Irish Catholic herself, she wanted Vivian to be educated as a lady. Roehampton had an excellent reputation for not only giving its pupils a fine scholastic background but also a cultural one. For instance if Roman history was the subject that year then everything else pertaining to the Roman Empire was studied from pottery, art, drama, literature and poetry. Besides, it was socially acceptable.

The school had a solid core of daughters drawn from the pre-Reformation great English families – the Howards, Arundells, Blundells, Wells, Tempests and Thunders. Added to these were the daughters of the Catholic diplomatic families and a few rank outsiders like Vivian Hartley and Maureen O'Sullivan who later became a Hollywood star. It was natural that the older families and the diplomatic daughters formed their own cliques and the outsiders like Vivian were made to feel slightly left out.

This may well have been the foundation of Vivien Leigh's social ambitions later in life. She was never shy of name-dropping.

Because she was perhaps the smallest, frailest and youngest child at the Convent, not only the older girls but the Sisters were inclined to pet her. Her pale, serious six-year-old face was such a long way away from her mother who had gone back to India.

One day there was special excitement when the Sisters announced the news that a huge wooden box had arrived for Vivian.

The Sisters entered into the whole spirit of the thing and the box was placed outside to be opened. All the pupils joined hands and danced out to the box where a sister began opening it.

The suspense was terrible. Suddenly the front fell down, the packing paper was unwrapped and there was a huge doll, but sadly the head had been broken in transit. All the small girls cried and little Vivian most of all.

Thoughtful Sisters phoned a relative and a new doll appeared fairly soon. It was some comfort but it was not the long-awaited doll from India.

Even as a child Vivien Leigh was thoughtful. The Viscountess Lambert (then Patsy Quinn), who was later to be her bridesmaid, remembers sitting down to Friday dinner of 'awful whiting with the tail in its mouth. Suddenly from the other table Vivien sent me a plate. It was salmon which her parents had sent her from Ireland and she wanted to share it with me.'

Discipline at Roehampton was martinet. The girls slept in small cubicles enclosed by white curtains. There was room only for a bed, chair and wash basin. At night the chair was placed in the corridor outside their curtains. On it each girl demurely placed her neatly folded underclothes shielded from the other girls' eyes by her white nightdress case. On top of this they were made to fold their stockings in the form of a cross.

To imaginative girls like Vivian Hartley it had a deep and mystic religious significance. But in fact it was the practical nuns' way of seeing that the stockings were properly aired each night.

After the cosseting of her home life in India where she had been cared for by a doting mother, English nurse and governess, life at the Sacred Heart Convent was a brusque experience. Even such a personal experience as the fortnightly hair washing took on a medieval ritual.

Because of her thick dark chestnut, aggressively curly hair, Vivian was sorted out with Maureen O'Sullivan, Dorothy Ward and Brigit Bolland for special treatment. These four 'thick heads' were scoured by the lay sisters to squeaks and protests before having their hair laid out on the special green chimney with its hot helmet lid. Every now and then the Sister lifted the helmet and to muffled moans shook the tangled tresses out and gave the scorched ears a draught of air.

Soon after she arrived at school Vivian Hartley had her long hair bingled. This was a cross between a shingle and a bob and was considered very daring by the girls from conventional families.

'But Vivian was always a pace-setter in fashion,' one of her school-friends says. 'When the rest of us arrived back from the holidays in stodgy "home clothes" and just longing for the anonymity of school uniform, Vivian always had an extra pretty wool dress with a little gold bracelet, special necklace and silk stockings.'

As Vivian grew older at school she and her friends formed a society for the beautiful ones, or 'exquisites', in contrast to the plain podges. They had a secret ritual that none of the other girls was allowed to know.

It was a magic play in which Vivian invariably played the rôle of the princess and the other exquisites took turns at being her prince. With the fairyland of childhood behind them they now yearned to be romantic.

Into this precocious world stormed Brigit Bolland who, unworthy of being a prince, elected to be a valiant swineherd. Seeing a bed of green daffodil spears piercing through the soil she proclaimed them to be 'a bed of steely nails' and to test her love for princess Vivian she promptly kicked off her shoes and walked through the spears slashing to the right and the left. A horrified princess shrieked with terror and fled before the wrath of the Reverend Mother descended.

There is a story that Vivian was an accomplice in putting black ink into the holy water in the nuns' chapel. But this sounds improbable. She had far too good manners as well as being too timid to behave so adventurously.

Even in her early teens Vivian Hartley was astonishingly beautiful. Her slender bones, appealing elfin-shaped face and blue-green eyes gave her a flower-like beauty. She was a perky Mustardseed in *Midsummer Night's Dream* but her first acting chance came when she was given the rôle of Miranda in *The Tempest*.

The play was a total disaster. On opening night Vivian's piping, flutey voice could not be heard further than the front row and she kept forgetting her lines. After the first act the producer, Brigit Bolland, was waiting in the wings in a furious rage. She picked up the nearest candlestick and beat Vivian over the head. For the rest of the play a terrified 'Miranda' hid in the flies in case she was attacked again.

Vivian Hartley was never a studious girl in the ordinary sense. Most lessons bored her and school reports invariably mentioned 'lack of concentration' and 'not keeping her mind on her work'. But she did enjoy dancing, drawing, playing the piano and violin and even played the 'cello in the school orchestra.

Her early background of bedtime reading with her mother in India – Hans Andersen, Charles Kingsley, Greek mythology and Kipling – had whetted her appetite to read. Apart from reading, visits to the theatre were her main interest and it is said that she held the schoolgirl record of seeing *Round in Fifty* at the London Hippodrome sixteen times. At this period George Robey was the man in her life.

During the holidays she used to travel to Ireland where the family had a fishing lodge. On the ferry she was often mistaken for Maureen O'Sullivan. Vivian took fun in hoaxing the passengers and carrying on a conversation as Maureen. It was the first signs of mimicry that became a party-special later in her life.

By the time she was thirteen it was quite obvious that Roehampton Convent was not the final solution for the education of Vivian Hartley. She was restless there and had not really found her niche. It was evident not only to the teaching Sisters but also to her family that she would be happier in other surroundings.

This fitted in with family plans as Mr and Mrs Hartley had arranged to do a small tour of Europe taking their daughter along with them. Mrs Hartley was an advanced and ambitious mother in every way and wanted her daughter to have a liberal outlook, perfect manners and the ability to converse fluently in the languages of the day that mattered – French, Italian and German.

The tour spread itself out for three years but during this time Mrs Hartley placed her daughter in various convents, affiliated with the Sacred Heart at Roehampton, along the coast – Dinard, Cannes, Biarritz, San Remo and then over into Salzburg and Zürich.

It was one of the most sensible things that any mother could have done because not only did this teenager end up speaking very good French and German but also reasonable Italian. Later she was able to dub her own films in German and French for showing in Europe which few English actresses have ever done. More than that she had developed in all the arts. Her passion for music, antiques and paintings later in life may well have stemmed from these early days of travelling.

Whenever school holidays permitted and she was in London Mrs Hartley took her daughter to see the various museums and art galleries. Even then Vivian loved everything that was physically beautiful and spent hours sightseeing with her mother. It was almost as if Mrs Hartley could foresee the future of her daughter's life, for this was no ordinary education usually given to middle-class daughters.

By now, at sixteen, Vivian Hartley needed only the final grooming to complete her education and Mrs Hartley chose Paris. It was a very small school at Auteuil which encouraged independence in the girls. They were allowed to wear their own clothes for most of the time and a few of the girls, including Vivian Hartley, even managed a little discreet make-up without attracting the wrath of the headmistress. She merely turned a blind eye.

French language and literature was still Vivian Hartley's main study but added to this was a course widely interpreted as drama. Several leading actresses were on call by the school to come and teach the students. Vivian's teacher was from the Comédie Française and considered one of the best.

After Christmas, spent with the family in Biarritz, Mrs

Hartley entered the last stage of her daughter's education. It was a small school on the Austrian-German border at Bayrisch-Gmain where again the accent was on culture and turning its pupils into international women who could take their place anywhere in the world and in any society.

Only a short train trip from Salzburg, the pupils were taken regularly to concerts and the opera. In later years Sir Malcolm Sargent, who became a close personal friend of the Oliviers during the war, said that he knew few non-professional musicians who had such a wide range of knowledge about music. 'We can talk for hours about music without ever getting bored with each other,' he said just before he died.

Though the last year had perhaps been one of the happiest in her school life Vivian was quite pleased to return to England just as she turned eighteen. She was longing to take up her old friendships and enjoy the London social life that she had never really known.

Though undoubtedly she would have made the news headlines as the most beautiful débutante in London, neither Vivian Hartley nor her parents were very interested in the idea. They had not lived in London permanently for many years and now had set up family life in a rented house in County Mayo. It was not until after her marriage that she was presented at Court.

Meanwhile, because there seemed no alternative to such a strong-minded young woman, Vivian had entreated her parents to allow her to study at the Royal Academy of Dramatic Art. She was only six when she first had confided to Maureen O'Sullivan at the Convent that she was going to be an actress.

It was at the South Devon Hunt Ball that Vivian Hartley met Leigh Holman. He came from a sound Dorset family and now had chambers in the Temple. His was a typical

English face that one encounters at Eton, Oxford, Hunt Balls, Henley, the Stock Exchange, Sotheby's, Boodles and the Travellers Club. It is not especially handsome but is strong, reliable, forthright and kind. It belongs to the type of man that mothers find an anchor for spirited daughters; these bachelors are worth their weight in pure gold.

Such a man was Leigh Holman – charming, educated, considerate, beautifully mannered and with good prospects. It was love at first sight as far as he was concerned and for the gay highly-spirited Vivian Hartley it was marvellous to have someone so considerate to pamper her. Most days he was waiting for her outside the Royal Academy when she finished classes and soon they became engaged.

The story goes that when Leigh Holman produced a sizeable diamond ring to celebrate their engagement Vivian gave him her sweetest smile and said:

'But, darling, where did you buy it?'

When he announced rather diffidently from Mappin and Webb she replied:

'But, Leigh, how extraordinary you are. Fancy going to a cutlery shop.'

In the rush of trousseau shopping and wedding plans Vivian Hartley dropped her classes at the Royal Academy. Though some of her friends thought it might be final, she confided to one of her classmates at the time: 'Just wait and see. I'll be back.'

And that is exactly what she did, just ten days after she had returned to London from her honeymoon.

'Had a Baby – a Girl'

IT WAS THE kind of marriage which was rewarding for any pre-war mother – 'establishment' and dependable. Friends congratulated Mrs Hartley on her son-in-law because he was adorably kind, generous and naïvely over-whelmed at his good fortune in securing such an exquisite bride.

They were married on 20th December 1932 at St James, Spanish Place, with all the trimmings of a 'nice wedding' of the thirties.

'All I remember was how thin and shy she looked,' a guest recalled. 'Yes, a shy little bride in white satin. The bridesmaids wore peach satin with puff sleeves and carried chrysanthemums. But it is her demureness that remains in my memory.'

The newly-weds left the reception at a London hotel in the usual cloud of confetti and kisses for a honeymoon in Switzerland.

On returning to London the new Mrs Holman and all the wedding presents moved into her husband's bachelor flat in Eyre Court, Finchley Road. There seemed no point at this stage in looking for a different place to live.

Their home life was conventional as suited Leigh Holman, a thriving young barrister. He had kept on his old house-keeper, Miss Adams, who ran the flat like clockwork. There was little for the new bride to do apart from arranging the flowers and a little shopping.

Lady Lambert, who as Patsy Quinn had been a brides-maid, remembers going to dinner there one night. She was early and stood in the drawing room talking to Vivian and waiting for Leigh Holman to arrive from the Temple.

'The front door key clicked and Vivian rushed for the door and flung her arms round the soldier-stiff Miss Adams who was just coming into the room. I shall never forget poor Vivian's blushes.'

All Vivian's girl friends, as they did all her life, found her enormous fun to be with.

'When Vivian rang up to do something that day, you knew you would have a marvellous time. She had a small car which she insisted on driving herself, putting the girl friend alongside her and Leigh Holman in the back. We used to whizz along, with Vivian exclaiming whenever she saw something in the shops that interested her. Leigh in the back seat would cover his eyes in horror.

'When Vivian was learning to drive she backed into a horse. An irate policeman came pounding up to her but she turned her full force of charm on him and he practically swooned on the spot.'

Just ten months after she was married and still in her nineteenth year Mrs Leigh Holman gave birth to a baby. In her pale blue diary she wrote: 'Had a baby – a girl.' That was all.

But to a girl friend who visited her in the nursing home she confessed: 'Never again – it is a messy business.'

It was soon pretty obvious that Mr Holman's bachelor flat was too small to accommodate a wife, housekeeper, nanny, himself and a new baby and so began the serious business of house hunting.

The Leigh Holmans finally chose what must have been one of the smallest houses in London. It was a Queen Anne dolls' house ranging over several floors in Little Stanhope Street near Shepherd Market. It even had a theatrical history as Lynn Fontanne had taken rooms there when she first acted in London. As far as Vivian was concerned this last romantic fact clinched the deal.

The family moved in and Vivian was enchanted to begin decorating her very first home. In the weekends the Holmans scoured the antique shops in Shepherd Market and round the countryside. Leigh Holman had a considerable knowledge of antiques and what Vivian did not know technically she made up for in her enthusiasm. They were a marvellously happy little family. There were small dinner parties, girls' lunches and cocktail parties and as any new bride knows the days were never long enough.

If it had not been for her extravagance in buying flowers and books (which she kept up all her life), and a single cigarette advertisement, Vivian Holman may never have seriously considered resuming her acting career.

A friend in advertising told her that they were looking for a beautiful girl to smoke a cigarette in an advertisement. The fee was small but it would cover the Bumpus book bill for a while. At the time Leigh Holman allowed her £200 a year dress allowance. More as a joke, Vivian put on her prettiest dress and went along for the interview. She was asked to hold the cigarette and stretch her head back. All her early life she had been embarrassed by her slender neck but it was this same willowy creamy neck, topped by her pert profile, that secured the cigarette job.

Within an hour several photographs had been taken and more work was promised. It had all been so easy.

Friends are still divided in their opinion. Some think that but for this splash of excitement and easily earned money she may have been content to forget acting and be a minor Mayfair hostess. Others differ. They reason that somewhere, somehow, she would have found a way to go back to her first love – acting. A normal married life would have bored her.

'I don't know if Leigh noticed it,' one friend remarked, 'but it was pretty obvious to all of us that she hated staying home and the stage seemed the obvious choice.'

To the guests who came for the small dinner or cocktail parties it seemed the perfect marriage. The ingredients were there – the beautiful young wife, the devoted older husband, and a well scrubbed, prettily plump baby brought in by nanny for inspection when she was required.

But the close and real friends knew that this marriage would never hold Vivian. She wanted excitement. She wanted to test herself in the outside world, and she hated the conventions of a normal marriage.

A girl friend who stayed with them at that time remembers coming home very late after a party and going into Vivian's bedroom. Her husband was away and she sat up in her big bed listening avidly to all the party gossip. At the end she pulled up her knees and putting her arms around them sighed:

'Oh, I feel so tied – so tied.' It was a remark that Scarlett O'Hara might have made.

In the August of 1933 the Leigh Holmans had planned to go on a yachting holiday in the Baltic. They were the envy of their smart young friends, but as the date grew nearer Vivian heard through a friend that Albert de Courville was looking for some young girls with good family backgrounds and acting experience for a film called *Things are Looking Up* with Cicely Courtneidge as the star. There was a slim chance that Vivian might be able to get a part.

As the date grew nearer and she had heard no word the Leigh Holmans left for Sweden where they were to join the yacht at Gotheburg. But before leaving Vivian had, much to her husband's amazement, made arrangements that if needed she could be contacted and she would return to

London. There was no use remonstrating that it would spoil the holiday. Vivian was adamant. Leigh Holman had come up against the same will power that many men were to experience in Vivien Leigh's lifetime.

At Copenhagen the cable arrived and after a fretful scene Vivian left for London. Leigh Holman finished the cruise alone and returned to find that the film was running behind schedule and as yet Vivian had not even been cast!

If he was resentful this quiet gentleman did not show it to friends and for her part Vivian became even more determined to get into the film. Her pride was now at stake.

In the thirties the well-brought-up débutante who wanted to work had fewer choices than now. If she was pretty and lively it was considered quite smart to go on the stage or try and get bit parts in films (it provided pin money but left plenty of time for social events and holidays). If she was skinny, to be a model at Molyneux was *de rigeur*. If plain, there were several snobbish flower shops who kept a gaggle of girls behind scenes wiring flowers, and if fat there was nothing left but to study music.

No one was more relieved than Vivian when the call came to attend a costume-fitting.

At the time she thought she was getting a small speaking part but this ended up as only a couple of lines. When the film was finally shown even these were cut, much to her annoyance.

Recalling these early days at Lime Grove Studio Anne Wilding (now Mrs Anne Adler of Lausanne, Switzerland) says, 'There was Judy Kelly, Gillian Maude, Hazel Terry, Vivian and me.

'We were given the part of schoolgirls in a typical comedy of the period. I first met Vivian in the dressing room. We had all gone for various fittings of our clothes previously and somehow up till now I had missed her.

'When I arrived Vivian was already in her clothes and looking very excited but I couldn't find mine. On looking round at all the other girls I realised that Vivian was the only one about the same size as me. After lots of searching and talking to the wardrobe mistress I finally asked Vivian if she was sure that these in fact were her clothes.

'Vivian assured me that they were her own. After a little while I asked her more pointedly to look in the back and see if her name was on them. With very good grace she took them off, looked, and saw "Anne Wilding". This was to be the beginning of a very close friendship.'

Though by nature a 'night owl' Vivien Leigh has never found it difficult to get up in the morning. Besides she now had the incentive of knowing that she was working. She was earning money and she had independence.

The location was Cobham Hall in Kent. There was an early morning studio bus that ran down from Lime Grove, but Vivian preferred to drive her own little car and asked Anne Wilding to share petrol expenses with her.

For two months in the summer they met every morning at six o'clock and set off. To while away the time when they were driving they would recite Shakespeare or sing. Their favourite songs were, *I am always happy when I am lying in the hay*, and *Your coffee in the morning*.

At first they used to sing in duet and then gradually got more ambitious and harmonised.

'We had a marvellous time,' Anne Wilding says. 'On rainy days we used to sit together and do *The Times* crossword puzzles. Vivian was always very quick and intelligent.'

This passion for crossword puzzles or word games stuck with Vivien Leigh for the rest of her life. There was scarcely ever a day when she was in England that she did not do *The Times* crossword.

Another affectation these girls had was the trick of raising one eyebrow. Like a naughty schoolgirl – and certainly not like a mother of a daughter – Vivian would sit in a corner and practise raising one eyebrow. Once she had found the trick she taught Anne and they would then do it in unison shrieking with laughter. Vivien Leigh later used this mannerism in many of her film rôles from Lady Hamilton and Scarlett O'Hara to Blanche de Bois and Mrs Stone.

The 'pug' game also amused them for hours between shots. Vivian taught Anne how to pull a hideous pug face and again they always ended up convulsed with giggles. Today it sounds childish and banal but this was a world when astronauts, hippies and the Pill were still fiction reading. It was thirty-four years ago.

The scene that really launched Vivian's film career was in a dormitory. Because of her piquant face and large luminous eyes she was the girl chosen to blow a raspberry at the mistress who came into the room. Small stuff maybe, but she was the envy of every other girl on the set.

Even then Vivian was to insist on every detail in her clothes being correct. Right through her career while always willing to listen to the costume designers' advice, she had always insisted that the first qualification of any costume she was to wear was that it flattered her. She had the same approach to stage appearance as Mrs Patrick Campbell.

In the film Anne Wilding recalls:

'We all wore prop pyjamas but Vivian asked to wear her own. They were conspicuous because they had "Vivling" embroidered on the left-hand side which was a family pet name and short for Vivian-darling.'

This may have been because she felt more comfortable in her own pyjamas but it is more likely that this was

Vivien Leigh's first calculated bit of scene stealing.

'In another scene we all had to wear panama hats with very high ugly crowns. After the first day I took mine home and had my mother cut the crown down so that it looked a little less pudding basin. It was such a success that next day Vivian asked if I would take hers home and have the same done.'

In the finished film Vivian and Anne had the satisfaction of seeing themselves distinguishable from the others by their sexy hats.

One of the scenes called for two girls to run around and receive shots from a tennis professional. Vivian and Anne volunteered but they were hopeless. It was much more difficult than it looked as the balls had to be played on a certain mark to catch the camera. They were quickly taken off that and the parts given to two other more sporty girls.

Whatever she thought privately of the ties of domesticity and being a mother, Vivian Leigh tried desperately hard to be just like the other girls and enjoy their fun. Anne had taken over a boy friend of Vivian's from before her marriage. Occasionally he would pick Anne up from the set and drive her to London. One day, to celebrate a birthday on the set, there was a party at the *Laughing Water* roadhouse just opposite the film studios. Vivian, who had not seen him for years, decided that it would be great fun if she rang him up pretending to be Anne. He was completely taken in and only when he arrived did he know of the deception.

'I remember one day,' says Anne Wilding, 'we were both looking through a movie magazine. We saw a picture of Laurence Olivier and I remarked I didn't like his eyebrows. I can't think why because now I think they are very nice. But Vivian thought he was tops.'

Vivian invited both Anne Wilding and Helen Terry to her twenty-first birthday – a cocktail party at the Holmans' house in Stanhope Street. Neither of them had been to a cocktail party before so they went to Swan and Edgars to fortify themselves with a good tea.

'We were worried that if we had a glass of sherry – or perhaps two – we might get tipsy.'

The party was crowded and an enormous success with Vivian looking very lovely in a blue-green dress that matched her eyes. But as yet she had not developed that difference that was to distinguish her from all the other chocolate-box beauties of the thirties.

It was a chance meeting at a cocktail party that led to Vivian's next step up. A friend of hers, actress Beryl Samson, found herself next to a young man, John Gliddon, who had been a journalist and was now setting himself up as an actors' agent. He told her of his plans – to find young, unknown beauties who could be trained into actresses and he wanted to handle them exclusively and groom them into top stars. He was convinced that this was the only way to get the star quality that Hollywood produced so successfully.

Beryl Samson listened fascinated and told him she had just the person to introduce to him – a girl of very exceptional beauty. This is how Vivian Holman came to go with Beryl Samson to Gliddon's new office in St John's Wood.

The interview was short and business-like. 'Now tell me, what experience you have had?' Gliddon asked.

'Well . . . I have been in a film. It's called *Things are Looking Up.*'

'What part did you play in it?'

'I had the part of a schoolgirl' – and here she smiled. 'I had two lines to say.'

'So you haven't really done much,' he said dampeningly.

'No – not really,' she answered honestly.

Gliddon some years after gave this version of how the

name Vivien Leigh was born. He had insisted that she changed her original name of Vivian Hartley because it did not sound sufficiently 'stagey'.

'What about Susanne Stanley,' suggested Vivian, 'or my maiden name Mary Hartley?' Neither she nor Gliddon at that first interview could reach an agreement. Later Gliddon went along to see Ivor Novello at the Palace Theatre. He took photographs of Vivian to show Novello.

'John, I think she is the most exquisite person I have ever seen.' He then told how only a few weeks before he had offered her a small part in his play *Murder in Mayfair* at a salary of £4 a week. She had turned it down saying: 'But I can get thirty shillings a day filming.'

'Then take the job, darling,' laughed Ivor. Which she did.

Gliddon then recalls that he and Ivor Novello wrote her name down on paper and suddenly Ivor said: 'Why not call her Vivien Leigh – half her husband's name and half her own.'

That, according to Gliddon, is how the name was born.

Convinced that Vivien Leigh's arresting beauty would get her a job even without much acting experience Gliddon began to take his new protegée round the various agents. While she herself was not too keen on this it was something to do and was amusing to tell her girl friends about.

In five weeks she was given her first film part in a quickie called *The Village Squire*. It took a week to make and Vivien was paid five guineas a day.

The next quickie, *Gentleman's Agreement*, was equally poor but it did lead to a part in *The Green Sash*, a play set in fifteenth-century Florence which was to be put on at the Q Theatre in Kew.

There was little time for rehearsals and Vivien was not experienced enough for the emotional scenes. But again her beauty scraped her through and Charles Morgan (considered at that time as powerful as the mighty James Agate) wrote in *The Times*, 'Her acting has precision and lightness which might serve her well when her material was of more substance.'

After one week she was offered a part in the film *Look Up and Laugh* which was being directed by Basil Dean and starring Gracie Fields.

For Vivien it was a terrifying experience as Basil Dean was known to be very tough on his young actors and actresses and did not suffer fools lightly. This was her first important part and she felt awkward and shy in front of the naked camera.

It was Gracie Fields who gallantly encouraged her by saying: 'Don't worry, love. You've got something.'

Recalling the film Gracie Fields says from her home in Capri:

'I am terribly sorry that I don't remember much about her except that she was a very, very lovely, intelligent girl, and she was always studying. I do remember she was learning Russian during the filming and this impressed me. I asked her, "Are you going over there?"

' "No," she said. "I just like to study different languages."

'She was nervous when Basil Dean was telling her how to do a scene. I used to tell her not to let it worry her and take no notice.

'I lost touch with Vivien for many years and about three years ago met her in Brighton with Gladys Cooper. It was really sad to see her ageing (which we all have to do). But when one is so beautiful it always seems so sad the bloom of youth has gone. I wanted to cry. The two most lovely women I've ever known together, one a lot older than the other.'

Actress Gladys Cooper is the step-mother of Vivien

Leigh's friend of the last seven years – Jack Merivale.

When the film was shown Vivien was bitterly disappointed. She had been badly lit and her swan neck looked out of proportion to her neat little head. When she was back at the same studios as a star years later the cameraman was reminded of his comments that her neck was too long.

'Well,' he said, 'she must have done something about it.'

James Agate once described this same neck as a tulip, adding that some tulips have 'too long stems'.

'It was a remark that had me worrying about my neck for years when I should have been worrying about my acting,' she said.

In latter years when swan necks had become accepted beauty, a direct result of the model girl cult, Vivien Leigh's neck was one of her greatest assets. In those early days Vivien had three faults to overcome despite her pretty face – her neck and how to use it, her sing-song elocution voice and her workmanlike hands.

For such a tiny, neat person she had strangely practical hands. It was not that they were only large for her size but with her slender wrists and small feet they looked incongruous.

Nobody was more painfully aware than Vivien herself who would stand at rehearsals with her arms tucked up underneath her armpits.

Elsie Fogarty used to boom at her during rehearsals and lessons: 'You look like a chicken going to roost.'

It was finally through reading Ellen Terry's autobiography that she was helped. She wore gloves at rehearsals so that she would be conscious of her hands and concentrate on moving them gracefully.

Even until the end of her career Vivien Leigh liked to wear gloves as often as she could in private life. On stage she had her dresses designed with specially long cuffs or flounces.

When people used to say to Vivien Leigh 'Of course it was easy for you with your beauty,' she used to be adamant.

'It didn't come easy. Nothing does. Nobody worked harder than I did on myself,' she would reply.

At the end of *Look Up and Laugh* Basil Dean decided that Vivien Leigh, though ravishingly pretty, was not good enough to keep on at Ealing. Had her contract been renewed she may have stayed in half-baked comedies for which she had neither the temperament nor talent instead of creating a sensation in her first West End play.

The First Success

15TH MAY 1935 was a normal day of the thirties. The weather was colder than usual and in some parts of England there were mid-winter temperatures. The Prince of Wales had invited Mrs Simpson as his guest to Ascot. Nudism was the new-found cult, with the waiters and maids at an exclusive club wearing nothing but loin cloths and aprons.

There were high spirits at the Cavendish Hotel where Rosa Lewis threw a champagne party celebrating the legal victory of Lord Revelstoke in a breach of promise case brought by Miss Angela Joyce – Miss England of 1930.

Kingsford Smith won a battle for his life when his propeller was damaged over the Tasman and Diana Napier in a soap advertisement said: 'Every girl should be taught this.' She had announced her engagement the day before to Richard Tauber.

There was a State ball at Buckingham Palace for Indian princes and the Maharajah of Kapurthala wore a tunic of cloth of gold studded with emeralds. T H Lawrence was unconscious at the Bevington Camp Military Hospital and Barbara Hutton had married Count von Haugwitz Revenlow, husband number two.

Marconi had produced a curious ray to put cars out of action and the Spurs had got a new manager.

Cigarettes cost 10 for 6d and 'a luxury house' was £449 freehold or 12s 6d weekly. Matheson Lang was opening in *Drake of England* and France told Moscow that 'Communist propaganda has got to stop'. Cecil Beaton had never looked before, or since, more beautiful.

This then was the world news span when Vivien Leigh opened in *The Mask of Virtue* at the Ambassadors and became 'famous overnight'.

The posters outside had her name up along with the other three established players – Lady Tree, Jeanne de Casalis and Frank Cellier. For the first time she saw her name spelt Vivien and not Vivian, a small but important detail that Sydney Carroll had insisted on.

'It sounds so much more feminine,' he said. Deep in his dedicated heart Carroll thought he had found a star before the curtain up but no one in the cast took it very seriously. Anna Neagle recalls today how Sydney Carroll originally wanted her for the part but Herbert Wilcox, to whom she was under contract, had planned for her to be in *Peg of Old Drury*.

It was all very exciting for Vivien Leigh but if she was nervous she did not show it to the rest of the cast. Her dressing room was filled with flowers and telegrams. Lady Tree had given her a whole set of The Yellow Book and Jeanne de Casalis (who carried the play) squeezed her arm for good luck.

There is a critical moment in every actor's or actress's life when no one can help them. It comes just that minute before he or she steps on to the stage for the first time. It is a kind of aloneness. Some players want to be near someone up to the last moment. Others chatter wildly to cover their nervousness. But Vivien had no peculiarities. 'If anything,' an actor who had played with her said, 'she became a little quiet. She never appeared to panic and she never seemed actressy.'

Just before the curtain went up Vivien remembered Lilian Braithwaite's advice – to take three deep breaths. It fills the lungs and calms the butterflies and was a habit that she kept all her acting life.

Later, when she became an international actress, Vivien Leigh invariably developed a nervous laryngitis the last week of rehearsals which oddly enough disappeared on the final dress rehearsal.

Marilyn Monroe had a kind of phosphorescence about her. Vivien Leigh had incandescence. Her light seemed to come from within. It was there unmistakably that first night. Whatever her technical shortcoming (her stage fall was nothing short of clumsy) her beauty shone out across the footlights and enslaved the audience from the first second.

At the end of the third act came the great test when Henrietta asks the Marquis to shoot her. The entire cast had been nervous for Vivien as this required experience as well as technical skill. She just got by but it did not matter. The audience was on her side all the way.

There were no single curtain calls and no speeches. Sydney Carroll did not approve of them. But the success of the play was established by the roar of applause. In the harsh light of today it was Vivien Leigh's delicate débutante beauty – so right for the mood at the time – that made her performance noticeable.

Immediately at the final curtain, Vivien's dressing room was inundated with family and friends. In those days it was even more of a vogue to go back stage where every star's dressing room was like a miniature flower shop. Presiding over the party was Mrs Hartley who proudly said:

'Vivien could have made a success of whatever she did.'

The family chose the fashionable Florida night club in Bruton Mews, off Berkeley Square, for their after-theatre celebration. It had a glass floor lit from beneath and the dashing innovation that the tables moved around the floor at the touch of a button. The Prince of Wales went there often.

In the party was Vivien and her husband, Leigh Holman,

and her parents, Mr and Mrs Hartley. They celebrated with champagne and danced till 4 am when they all dashed to Fleet Street to see what the morning papers said.

The critics were unanimous – a new star had been found. 'Vivien Leigh shines in a new play' . . . 'New Star to win London' were typical headlines.

The critic of the *Evening News* wrote: 'At her first entrance Miss Vivien Leigh as the baggage was seen not only to be very pretty but to have the perfect air of false demureness. But she is only a charming beginner.'

In the *Daily Mail*, Willson Disher said: 'She has youth, beauty and assurance the part of Henrietta requires. In addition she has a boldness in attack which wins our whole-hearted admiration. She should go a long way indeed.' It was the kind of 'first' that every young actress dreams about.

Hardly had Vivien got to bed at daybreak than the gossip reporters were round at the little house in Stanhope Street. She was photographed in a cheesecake pose sitting in demure tennis shorts on top of piles of cushions playing a banjo. Oddly enough this photograph today has a decidedly amateurish quality about it. There were pictures in a fashionable cloque coat with shoulder collar of black fox and holding her small daughter Suzanne.

It was the full star treatment and Vivien Leigh handled herself with aplomb. In an interview in the *Daily Mail* titled 'Vivien Leigh on "How I Did It"' Margaret Lane wrote: 'This tiny, slender-boned little creature with the grey eyes and delicate heart-shaped face, has more responsibilities on her shoulders than most women twice her age would care for. She is able to take them lightly and yet competently because – having had marriage and motherhood and stardom thrust on her before she was twenty – she has had to solve a problem that has wrecked the lives of women far more experienced than herself.

'She has learnt the trick of combining marriage with a strenuous career.'

Sydney Carroll had thought that nineteen sounded a much better age than twenty-one. So he had deliberately lopped off a couple of years from Vivien's correct age.

With three small parts in 'quickies' in a London film studio and one play as her total acting experience Vivien Leigh conducted the interview like a veteran.

' "It was a very arduous regime," she said talking and winding up the clockwork pig for Suzanne at the time. "I had to leave the house by six or seven every morning when I was filming, and part of the time I was rehearsing and playing at the [Kew] theatre as well.

' "I had to run the house by a sort of correspondence course with my housekeeper – I'd leave her a note last thing about the baby and the next day's meals, but I'd be gone before she got up in the morning.

' "Then she'd leave me notes before she went to bed which I'd get when I got home late at night. There simply wasn't any leisure, and my husband and I hardly ever saw each other at all. That was rather awful of course but he was as much interested in my getting on as I was, and was very nice and put up with it."

' "Well then," she says, winding the pig up for the eighth time and steadying Suzanne on her feet, "you know the rest . . . it's the most exciting thing that ever happened to anybody. I didn't sleep at all last night, but sat up till four in the morning to see the newspaper notices, and of course when I'd seen them there was no going to sleep then!" '

Miss Lane described Vivien Leigh as 'a young suburban young lady' but continued in lyric style:

'As for her future, which appears to be one of the

rosiest that ever confronted a beautiful and determined young woman of nineteen – "Of course I shall go on working," she says, "this is only a beginning. I always meant to have a stage career, and I married on that understanding. You can be happily married and work terribly hard at something else you know – I certainly am and do. Though perhaps" – and here she paused to take a crushed cigarette out of Suzanne's clenched hand and a match out of her mouth – "if it hadn't been for the unselfishness of Nannie and my wonderful housekeeper it might not have been so easy after all." '

'Mr Holman is tall with fair hair and has the keen, energetic-looking face of the typical barrister. He said to a *Daily Mail* reporter:

' "You must not ask me to give an opinion of the performance. I do not think it is my place to discuss it." '

This was the beginning of Vivien Leigh's star-studded career. From then on she had few failures, never knew the agony of doing the agents' rounds, and she seldom played a part she didn't want to. It was starlight all the way. . . .

Carroll and Korda

ALTHOUGH SOME CREDIT for seeing the star qualities in Vivien Leigh must go to John Gliddon, the actor's agent with whom she had signed up, it was Sydney Carroll who made her a star overnight. He had already seen her at the Q Theatre in *The Green Sash* and marked her down for future use when the right play turned up.

This amazing man was a character of the thirties. He had the extraordinary position of not only being a very highly respected theatre critic for the *Daily Telegraph* but also a producer of considerable standing. The money he made from his writing, and buying up small magazines which he later sold at a profit, was immediately sunk in his theatre productions. He was the first to begin the open-air theatre at Regent's Park – a precarious investment in a wet summer. Not all his productions were successful but they were the means of many interesting young actors and actresses getting a lift up.

He had panache and great kindliness and whereas James Agate was dreaded for his stinging pen and Charles Morgan for his cool caution, Sydney Carroll was benevolent to young actors and actresses.

In writing after the first night of *The Mask of Virtue* about his discovery of Vivien Leigh he was positively lyrical:

'I congratulate myself upon having encountered on the threshold of her career a young girl whose mental balance of mind equals her physical poise, one who can bring a divine sense of humour to meet the many vicissitudes and setbacks that are certain to be her accompaniments to fortune so long as she pursues it.

'Vivien Leigh as an actress and a potential "star" of high rank may have a great deal to learn, but at least she is ready and anxious to acquire all the knowledge about her profession that she can. Her personality is charming in the extreme but its possessor realises that something more than personality is called for in the struggle up the ladder, and nothing will be left undone by her to attain perfection as absolute as it can be found.

'It is grand to think that Old England can turn out all this promising material out of which we hope to see emerge the Bergners, the Bernhardts and the Duses of the future.

'The ambitious beginner needs plenty of nerve, power of attack, power of retention, control of body and mind, imagination, sensibility, judgment, clear diction, sense of timing, regard for variety and a love of repose. Throw in as well beauty of figure and face, glory of voice, breadth of movement and sublety of brain, and what critic can withstand the appeal?

'It would seem grossly unfair that any one person should be blessed with all these merits I have enumerated but it sometimes happens and when it does fame comes "in a night" and small wonder.

'I gave her her chance without seeing any press notices, photos, or pictures. I was influenced solely by my own judgment plus a knowledge of palmistry. Vivien allowed me to read her hands and her remarkable line of success or destiny struck me as being unique.'

Sydney Carroll was right in predicting that nothing would be left undone by Vivien Leigh to attain perfection, for this professionalism was the strongest point in her career. She became an actress of intellect and not of heart. Technically she could not often be faulted within her own limits but emotionally and spiritually she rarely attained greatness.

He was also wrong in predicting 'the many vicissitudes and setbacks that are certain to be her accompaniments to fortune'.

Of all actresses Vivien Leigh had few setbacks. The only man to resist her was David Selznick when he did not choose her for the rôle in the film *Rebecca*. She longed to play the timid pale wife to Olivier's Max de Winter. She was given several tests for the rôle but when she appeared on the screen the Hollywood director thought she looked 'foxy'.

When told of his verdict Vivien snapped, 'Foxy indeed!'

During rehearsals for *The Mask of Virtue* all had not been well. Mrs Sydney Carroll recalls that the producer, Maxwell Wray, was not altogether happy with Vivien in the part of Henrietta and had complained to Sydney Carroll of her restlessness and her lack of repose. She also had some irritating mannerisms and her voice was far from strong.

Sydney Carroll took the matter in hand himself. He was determined that she would be a success. He undertook to coach her in how to sit, walk, use her hands and, the most important of all, relax.

His pupil was so quick to learn that on the opening night when the curtains parted on the scene when Henrietta is sitting in her black velvet gown looking demure, graceful and coolly beautiful the audience gasped.

Nicolas Carroll, Sydney Carroll's son, remembers the play clearly:

'It must have been in my summer holidays just after *The Mask of Virtue* opened that I came up from school and my father gave me a ticket to see the play. My memory of Vivien was of this extraordinary swan-like neck of hers with the head rather gracefully balanced.

'Being young and inexperienced about women this

44

arrested my attention very much. I remember my father taking me round back stage afterwards to meet her. She was all painted up, of course, and it was a slight loss of glamour for me to see her in her theatre paint.'

All through her life Vivien Leigh kept in touch with Sydney Carroll. She and Laurence Olivier used to have yearly lunches or dinners at the Ivy or the Savoy, Sydney Carroll playing the rôle of the proud benefactor and she the gracious star.

'I remember hearing about Vivien's last visit to my father,' says Nicolas Carroll. 'He was then in his middle eighties and I am sorry to say that he was dying.

'He had had two strokes and his third stroke was not very far off. Vivien Leigh heard about his illness and wrote to ask if she could come and visit him.

'She sat by his bedside and they had a lunch of chicken-something together. She was very kind to him and I think she was genuinely moved to see this old man who had been good to her. She allowed pictures of them to be taken for the newspapers and this seemed to please my father.'

Whether in fact Sydney Carroll did honestly believe over the years that Vivien Leigh had attained the status of Sarah Bernhardt he would never allow a word of criticism about her.

'The only other time I remember talking to my father about Vivien Leigh I am sorry to say that I upset him very much by telling him a story that I had heard from my former wife who was Polish.

'Vivien Leigh and Laurence Olivier were in Poland and their host had taken them to a dinner party at one of the major hotels. Half way through the dinner there was a sudden scream from Vivien and it appeared that she had lost a piece of jewellery. Great tragedy, great consternation. She may have left it in her bedroom or lavatory or somewhere like that, but she put everyone into a fuss.

'To come back to my father. I told him the story. Not harshly but I could see that I was on the wrong tack. I was sitting by his bedside and he was growing increasingly red in the face and upset. The strokes had affected his speech but gradually he blustered out:

' "I don't believe it. It is not true. It is very wicked of you to tell the story."

'You see, even in his middle eighties he still had this warm protective feeling for her. She was a symbol in his life. She symbolised a certain sort of glamour and success and the only other woman in which he got similarly involved, though not so deeply, was Victoria Hopper.

'But the difference was of course that he really thought that Vivien Leigh was a great actress. For him she was in the Sarah Bernhardt tradition. He was very non-critical about her and on the few occasions that I ventured to suggest that her success in *Gone With the Wind* and *Streetcar* were due to brilliant direction he became quite cross and said:

' "Oh no, no! A director can do nothing without a first-class actress." '

Right till the day of his death Sydney Carroll wanted to know all the news about Vivien Leigh and Laurence Olivier. As far as he was concerned there never would be anyone like them again and there would certainly never be another Vivien.

It had been the kind of dress-up glittering first night that London excels in. Sydney Carroll had seen that all the right people packed the stalls to see his protegée, Vivien Leigh.

Among those who called backstage after the first act was Alexander Korda, the Hungarian expatriate who was one of the most stimulating and influential figures in the film industry. He was not only the most sought-after director, because of his successful production of *The Private Life of Henry VIII*, but it was known that he was a woman's director. He knew and understood them and, like most Hungarian charmers, women bloomed in his presence.

Vivien Leigh had been taken to see him by John Gliddon a few weeks before, but Korda saw nothing electric or unusual in the keen slim girl in front of him. It was the usual in-out interview with faint-hearted promises for a screen test in the future. They had left the building sad and silent.

'Don't worry, Vivien,' Gliddon said. 'The day will come when they will all want you, I promise.'

But now it was different. Korda, too, had been mesmerised by Vivien's beauty. Behind stage it was arranged that Gliddon should call on him the next day to discuss a contract.

Even before *The Mask of Virtue* had opened, the grapevine (fanned by the energetic Carroll) had been busy and Hollywood agents had already been alerted to a possible 'sensational discovery'.

By the time Gliddon had arrived at his office to see what the mail had bought, before going on to see Korda at Isleworth Studios, there had been phone calls from every important film company in Britain.

But both Vivien and her agent wanted to tie up with Korda and no one else. They both thought that if anyone could handle her new career he could. And they were right.

This time at Isleworth there was no waiting and Gliddon was shown into Korda's office on arrival. Korda came to the point. He wanted to put Vivien on his pay roll at £10 a week – the same terms he had given Merle Oberon. Then began the bargaining.

Gliddon knew that Vivien Leigh felt passionately that she must continue with the theatre as it would give her a chance to improve her acting technique. He suggested to Korda that his film contract was only valid for six months of each year, leaving her free for the theatre for the rest of the year.

Korda, also a shrewd bargainer, put on a show of impatience and wanted the contract signed immediately.

'I don't bargain,' he snapped. 'And I am very busy.'

Gliddon, poker faced and dead cool, replied:

'Give me twenty-four hours to think it over,' and left.

Next morning, feeling sure of his ground, Gliddon phoned Korda and said:

'Sorry I can't accept the terms of contract. Vivien Leigh is going to be a great star.'

'How much do you want?' said Korda.

An hour later the contract of £1500 a year for six months filming was signed, with Korda reluctantly agreeing to pay her £1800 for two films in the fifth year. It was a British record for a new-born star.

It was a harassed and excited Gliddon who rushed to the first telephone box to tell Vivien, who was waiting at home, the marvellous news.

That evening the newspaper posters announced a £50,000 contract for Vivien Leigh and though in fact it was thousands out in value it had begun the legend – the star quality of Vivien Leigh.

Vivien was wildly excited as she realised that she was firmly on her way. She never doubted that now it was merely a question of time and hard work and she would be at the top. Her husband Leigh Holman was somewhat stunned. This had not been quite what he had planned when he married his beautiful demure bride. With his legal background and appreciation of money it all sounded

Vivian Hartley in
Ireland where the
family went for
holidays during
the 1920's.

Courtesy of Lady Lambert

Four star performers of the tennis courts at Roehampton School in 1928: Vivian
Hartley is on the extreme right, Patsy Quinn, now Lady Lambert, is second from
the left.

Courtesy of Lady Lambert

The portrait (*top*) was taken by Antony Beauchamp when he was sixteen and Vivian Hartley was nineteen. The lower photograph was taken when, as Mrs Leigh Holman, she was presented at Court.

astonishing. If up till then he had not taken Vivien's career seriously, now was the time to think again. His private thoughts on how it would affect their domestic life he kept to himself. Nothing must hinder Vivien on her first step to stardom.

But Vivien had yet to learn the deadening procrastination of the film industry. Months went by and no word from Korda. He was engrossed building his new studios at Denham and Vivien was in effect just another name in his stable of stars in the making.

Despite all Sydney Carroll's energies to publicise *The Mask of Virtue* it was not the success that it promised. When he transferred it from the cosy atmosphere of the Ambassadors to the twice as large St James he even showered London with thousands of pin-up postcards of his *Star in a Night* girl.

The play in fact ran only four months. Out of work again Vivien was becoming restless when there came an offer from Leslie Howard for her to play Ophelia to his *Hamlet* on Broadway. At the same time Korda was toying with the idea of making *Cyrano de Bergerac* with Charles Laughton and wanted Vivien for Roxanne.

Acting under Gliddon's instructions, Vivien cabled Leslie Howard asking if he would wait for a few weeks until Korda reached a decision and Howard agreed.

In the meantime she was tested for Roxanne. The studio had asked her to dye her hair blonde but even in those days Vivien Leigh had a touch of imperialism. She would not do anything against her will and suggested a compromise of a blonde wig. In fact the only time in her career when she was persuaded to dye her hair blonde was for Laurence Olivier's stage production of *A Streetcar Named Desire* when she felt freedom of movement was essential.

Finally word came that *Cyrano* was being dropped as Korda and Laughton were at cross purposes and could not agree about anything, ranging from false nose to script.

Vivien cabled Leslie Howard immediately but it was too late. He had made other plans. It was her first major disappointment. To have made Broadway in her first year, playing opposite so skilled an actor as Leslie Howard, was any young actress's dream.

By December 1935 Vivien was becoming desperate. Seven months had gone by since she had been 'discovered' and there was still no sign of the stardom that Korda had promised her. She already knew that the fickle theatre public would lose interest unless she did something else soon to keep her name alive.

It was then that Ivor Novello, who was captivated by her beauty, had offered her the part of Jenny Mere in his production of Max Beerbohm's *The Happy Hypocrite*.

But even this she could not accept as it came inside the six months, which in her contract with Korda had to be reserved for making his films. Apart from this she had signed a stage contract with Sydney Carroll that he had an option over her for the next play.

Vivien Leigh and her husband spent the New Year at the *Lygon Arms* in Broadway in the midst of the peaceful Cotswolds' country. They both needed to get away from London, enjoy the country air and plan for the future.

On New Year's day Vivien wrote an agitated letter from Broadway to Gliddon saying that she felt it was vitally important that she should soon work again. She wanted to work for Novello because she felt she would learn much from him and he would be sympathetic to her.

The prospect of filming by day, acting in the theatre at night and being a wife and mother did not dismay her. 'It will be a wonderful experience and just what I want,' she wrote.

Few people could resist Vivien's beauty and enthusiasm

and even Korda relented in her contract.

As there were still two months to go before rehearsals, Vivien Leigh accepted John Gielgud's invitation to go up to Oxford and play in *Richard II*. It was the policy of the Oxford University Dramatic Society to use professional actresses for the female rôles.

Undergraduate David King-Wood played Richard II, Michael Denison had some minor parts and Byam Shaw and Gielgud directed. Vivien and Max Beerbohm's wife, Florence Kahn, were the only professionals.

Looking back Michael Denison says:

'I was utterly enslaved by her beauty. We all were.'

Max Beerbohm was to remark with some enthusiasm:

'Miss Vivien Leigh's performance was of exquisite sensibility – a foreshadowing of how much to come in later years!'

After the final night there was a gay supper party ending up at the Randolph Hotel in Oxford. No one wanted to go to bed, Vivien least of all. Fourteen of the cast decided to drive to Burford, a sleepy stone town in the Cotswolds, and have breakfast.

Back in London Vivien threw herself into Novello's production. Just what went wrong is lost in time but *The Happy Hypocrite* came off after only a few weeks leaving Vivien Leigh free, disappointed and again restless. Sydney Carroll rescued her and put her in *Henry VIII* which he was staging in Regent's Park. The enamoured Mr Carroll had not taken into account Vivien's yet undeveloped voice and though she looked a dream flitting in and out of the shrubs her voice was in fact hardly audible. As one critic gallantly commented: 'Vivien Leigh is on the slight side for park acting.'

One year had gone by, but now at last came word that the mighty Korda was ready.

Olivier

'It was like magic to see them together,' actors' agent Dorothy Mather recalls. 'They were so in love that they gave out a special atmosphere.'

She was referring to Vivien's first film with Laurence Olivier, *Fire Over England*, which they made together in 1937, a few months after they had met.

'At Denham it was accepted that everyone sat together at the big lunch tables and there was no pairing off to have a gossip. But with Vivien and Larry it was different. They sat alone completely immersed in each other and no one dreamed of going to join them. There was this great empty space around them.'

Neither Vivien Leigh nor Laurence Olivier could pinpoint exactly the date they first met. Only that it was during the four months when Vivien was playing in *The Mask of Virtue*.

Vivien had acquired the theatrical habit 'to see and be seen' and frequently dined out after the performance either at the Savoy or the Ivy as these two restaurants were frequented by the theatre hierarchy.

This night she was escorted by John Buckmaster, Gladys Cooper's son, who was one of the many young men at the time enslaved by her beauty. At a nearby table sat Laurence Olivier and his wife, Jill Esmond.

Buckmaster made some disparaging remark about Olivier looking odd without his moustache. And just as she had defended his eyebrows to her girl friend, Anne Wilding, a few months earlier, Vivien flew to Olivier's defence.

'I don't think he looks a bit odd,' she said, 'in fact I think he looks rather nice.'

All four were to meet up for a few minutes in the foyer where Vivien met Laurence Olivier for the first time.

By now it was an accepted thing in the Leigh Holman household that theatre people would inevitably become their new friends. It was, therefore, quite natural that the Oliviers asked the Holmans to lunch at their house at Burchett's Green, near Maidenhead.

Had she been asked at the time, she probably would have denied it, but Vivien was fully aware during that lunch of Laurence Olivier's magnetism. The moment that two people, destined to be lovers, first become aware of each other, there is magic in the air.

Vivien persuaded Ivor Novello to take her to a matinée at the Lyric Theatre to see Olivier in *Bees on the Boatdeck*, in which he played with Ralph Richardson. It was a sultry steaming day and the theatre was having a heatwave famine. They sat in a box and Vivien never took her eyes off Olivier the entire performance. A few days later Vivien Leigh and Laurence Olivier lunched together, alone.

In later years it amused Vivien to tell the story how she and a girl friend went to see Olivier in *The Royal Family*, and she whispered, 'That's the man I'm going to marry.'

'Don't be stupid – you are both married already.'

'It doesn't matter. I will still marry him one day. You see.'

Sir Alexander Korda, who later was to be such an influence in Vivien Leigh's life, announced plans for filming A E W Mason's *Fire Over England*. Vivien was thrilled. It not only gave her a chance to work under the eminent German film director, Erich Pommer, but she had also heard that Olivier was to be in the cast. Flora Robson was to play Queen Elizabeth I, Vivien the rôle of

Cynthia, the Queen's lady-in-waiting. To introduce 'box office', a fictitious part of Cynthia's lover was created in the film, and this Olivier was to play.

They met on the set for the first time in the corridor outside the self-help canteen.

Vivien politely remarked how nice it was that they were working together. Olivier laughed and replied, 'People always get sick of each other when making a film – we shall probably end up by fighting.'

In between scenes Olivier and Vivien used to walk along the paths in the gardens or visit each other's dressing rooms. When there was time, they used to steal away to a nearby pub.

'Whether they thought they were fooling anybody, I don't know,' says a member of the set crew. 'But we all knew that here were two people hopelessly in love. We used to call them "the lovers".'

With Flora Robson omnipresent in the film, neither Vivien Leigh nor Olivier had much of a chance. The most one could say of them was that they looked decorative and that their love scenes had the right touch of authenticity.

There has always been a mystery about how Vivien Leigh came to join the Old Vic and play Ophelia in the *Hamlet* the company took to Denmark in 1937. The answer, according to Robert Jorgensen of the Danish Tourist Association who inspired the idea of the visit, is that Laurence Olivier asked for her.

Robert Jorgensen was the dashing publicist engaged by Sydney Carroll to handle *The Mask of Virtue*. It was he who had marshalled the Press swarming outside the Holmans' house in the morning after Vivien's West End début. This idealist had always cherished the dream of seeing *Hamlet* played where Shakespeare set his tragedy, at

Kronborg Castle in Elsinore, along the coast from Copenhagen. And when Olivier fresh from his success in films joined the Old Vic Company to play *Hamlet* in a full-length unconventional production under Tyrone Guthrie, Jorgensen saw his dream becoming a possibility.

He discussed the idea with the Danish Tourist Board who were quick to grasp its possibilities as a summer tourist attraction, then he approached Lilian Baylis and Guthrie who, apart from the sheer mechanics of staging a play in the courtyard of a castle, were fascinated.

Two changes had to be made in the company. Because of previous commitments, Anthony Quayle took over from Michael Redgrave as Laertes and a substitute had to be found for Cherry Cottrell as Ophelia. It was then, according to Robert Jorgensen, that Laurence Olivier asked Lilian Baylis to invite Vivien Leigh to join the company for this trip. Technically Vivien was under contract to Sydney Carroll, but he was delighted that his adored protégée be given the chance to act with a company of such high standards and Jorgensen, who was still working for Sydney Carroll, arranged the special invitation from the Danish Government for her.

The British Council gave Jorgensen a £400 grant towards expenses and the Danish shipping line and railways offered to carry the cast free. The Marienlyst Hotel invited the Old Vic Company to be their guests and the actors agreed to the ridiculous salary of £20 each for their services. A special charter plane from London flew over during the week with a sprinkling of celebrities.

Learning a script in record time had never been difficult for Vivien Leigh who had been taught pelmanism as a child. Laurence Olivier used to rehearse her in the car on their way to and from Denham where they were both filming *The First and the Last*.

In the early rehearsals Tyrone Guthrie was irritated by many of Vivien's mannerisms, the same that had annoyed the director of *The Mask of Virtue*. He found her movements 'much too pretty' and 'much too dainty', and she was inclined to trip about the stage. The fear that her voice was not strong enough for an outdoor performance was overcome anyway as the platform at Elsinore was wired with amplifiers.

After two days of rehearsing in pouring rain under umbrellas in the castle forecourt, the final dress rehearsal had to be abandoned because of the weather.

Two thousand seats had been erected for the public, who were coming from all over Denmark. The last English company to play at Kronborg had been in 1585, and the interest for this company had been fantastic. At six o'clock on the day of the performance the wind from the Kattigat was so strong and the rain still lashing down that a decision had to be made.

As Robert Jorgensen recounts: 'We decided to move the whole performance to the ballroom of the Marienlyst Hotel which is a kilometre away from the castle. Everybody worked furiously and a stage was created merely by the placing of the chairs around the empty space.

'I remember just before the performance was to begin three of our senior theatrical critics were having drinks and said to me: "Boy, you have a terrific flop on your hands. It can't be done."

' "You don't know the sporting instinct of the British," I replied.'

Vivien was too concerned as to whether she was a good enough Ophelia to Olivier's Hamlet to be worried and in any case the ballroom was more suitable for her voice. But Laurence Olivier seemed to revel in the new challenge and spent a frantic two hours working out with the cast the various entrances and exits. Forty Danish officer cadets had been called in as extras and they had to be given explicit instructions how to walk in step carrying the dead Ophelia. But so good was the acting and the spirit behind it that many of the noble Danes there, including the present King and Queen, instead of feeling they had been cheated, felt that they were seeing Shakespeare in the kind of setting for which it was originally written. There was one problem in that Prince Knut sat in the front row with his long legs stretched out in front of him. The sword fights had to be conducted round them until he retrieved them in the interest of safety.

It was a sensational evening, the cast and audience seemed to flow together in this intimate setting. As Ivor Brown of *The Times* said, it was as good a performance of *Hamlet* as he had ever seen.

The Danish Press were ecstatic. No play has ever received more press in Denmark. There were no reviews but each paper carried two or three pages of souvenir photographs. Olivier had enchanted the Danes with his virile masculine Hamlet and Vivien Leigh's beautiful Ophelia stunned everyone.

The next evening under a cold Northern sky, with everyone of the 2000 chairs occupied, the company played within the castle courtyard. After the performance there was a party at the Old Town Hall.

All through the week the hospitable Danes had arranged various lunches but all the company wanted was to be left as much free time as possible.

Though there was no hint of it in the Danish Press the entire company knew that Vivien and Larry were wildly in love.

With the excitement of *Hamlet at Elsinore* still in their

minds, Vivien Leigh and Laurence Olivier returned to London at the end of June 1937 to face a very personal decision.

In Denmark they had agreed that they could no longer live apart and that Jill Esmond and Leigh Holman would have to be told of their decision. In each case it was painful.

Just a few weeks before, Jill Esmond had given birth to a baby son whom they called Tarquin. She was resting from the theatre and immersed in caring for her baby.

It was, in effect, the same tragic situation that was to happen to Vivien Leigh twenty-five years later. For Leigh Holman the decision was cruel but perhaps less of a surprise. With his kindly insight he had been an indulgent husband as he watched his shy bride bloom into an exotic beauty who was determined to become an actress of importance.

He knew that Vivien was completely intoxicated with the theatre and that there was no way back to normal married life. Added to this was the undeniable glamour and showmanship of Laurence Olivier who was then at the height of his physical attraction.

It was not that Vivien Leigh and Leigh Holman were unhappy together. It was merely that they had completely different temperaments – and now completely different worlds.

When Vivien told Leigh Holman of her decision to live with Laurence Olivier there were no recriminations on his part. Whatever his private grief there was no criticism. He did everything he could to make the parting easier for everyone.

Baby Suzanne remained with him until Vivien's mother, Mrs Hartley, took her to Canada during the war years. It was not until the last ten years of Vivien's life that Suzanne, now Mrs Robin Farrington, and her mother were to become real friends and know each other intimately.

For the rest of her life Vivien Leigh and her first husband were to remain the closest of friends. Ironically it was to him that she turned for comfort and understanding when her marriage with Laurence Olivier broke up.

In theatrical circles, with their acceptance of such situations, it was now completely acknowledged that Vivien and Larry were together.

To begin their new life they went to Venice for a short holiday. With her love of paintings and inquisitive mind, Vivien was in a dream as she went from church to art gallery. In the evenings they wandered hand in hand through the narrow streets. Life had never been more wonderful.

'I have never seen two people more in love in my life,' a friend recalls. 'Vivien was always unbelievably beautiful, but when she returned from Venice there was something different about her. It was as though she had found a deeper meaning to life. She was less nervous and simply could not take her eyes off Larry.'

Back in London Vivien Leigh was loaned immediately to MGM to make *A Yank at Oxford*. At first she did not want to make the film and always said in later years that it was not a particularly happy time. A contemporary at the Roehampton Convent, Maureen O'Sullivan, and Robert Taylor were to co-star. It is a long time ago and people's minds are dimmed but it is said that the two girls did not get on as well as they might have. The only person to enjoy the film was Robert Taylor.

It was not an important part in Vivien Leigh's career, as seen on the whole, but she did give a credible performance as the popsy wife of the Oxford bookseller. Scorpion-born as she was she brought a sting in the tail to her characterisation.

During this period Laurence Olivier was engrossed in

the Michael Saint-Denis production of *Macbeth* for the Old Vic. The American actress Judith Anderson was brought over from New York to play Lady Macbeth. In those early days of her career Vivien Leigh could never have coped with the dramatic range the part required and was the first to realise this. Apart from a performance that didn't satisfy her at Stratford-on-Avon in 1955, she never again managed to play *Lady Macbeth*. This, because of her individual and original conception of the part, is a great loss to the British theatre. It is one of the few Shakespearean rôles that she had really studied and hoped to play in the years ahead.

When Olivier's film of *Macbeth* fell through, in which she would have had a chance to show her very unorthodox approach, she said: 'I wanted more than anything else to film *Macbeth* with Larry. Tragedy is far easier to act in than comedy and I feel only now I really understand the character of Lady Macbeth.'

In memory of the film that never was Laurence Olivier gave his wife a ruby ring with an arrow through it which was one of her favourite pieces of jewellery.

Towards Christmas of 1937 the Old Vic staged *A Midsummer Night's Dream* and Tyrone Guthrie chose the fragile looking Vivien as Titania. The whole production was a fairy romp with the flying ballet in Victorian ballet skirts garlanded with red sashes and pink Oliver Messel roses. The part of Oberon was played by the Australian ballet dancer Robert Helpmann in his first speaking part, and Ralph Richardson was Bottom.

It was the beginning of a close friendship with Robert Helpmann that was to extend to Vivien Leigh's death. In latter years he was to direct some of her greatest successes, *The Duel of Angels* and *La Dame aux Camelias* and her last play *La Contessa* which did not make the West End.

A couple of months after *A Midsummer Night's Dream* had been running there was a call from Buckingham Palace that the Queen was bringing the two little princesses – then eleven and seven – to a matinée. During the interval Titania, Oberon and Bottom were taken to the rear of the Royal Box to meet the princesses. As Vivien and Robert Helpmann retired their spectacular head-dresses became entangled and nearly bursting with laughter they almost crawled backwards until they were able to get disentangled round a corner and collapse into giggles.

When asked to contribute towards this book, Robert Helpmann wrote: 'I must ask you to forgive me but from a personal point of view I can only say that the loss of Vivien has been one of the great blows in my life and I feel it too close and far too personal even to discuss.'

Why was Vivien Leigh, a relatively unknown English actress, chosen to play the coveted part of Scarlett O'Hara in *Gone With the Wind*? It was a rôle that every American film actress wanted and among those who had seriously been considered were such established stars as Katharine Hepburn, Bette Davis, Susan Hayward, Joan Fontaine, Norma Shearer, Margaret Sullivan, Paulette Goddard, Talullah Bankhead and even Lucille Ball of *I Love Lucy*.

According to director George Cukor, who had been working for a year preparing the film, the reason that Vivien was chosen was that not only did she look ravishingly pretty but she was 'fresh and not shop worn'. She was unknown to American audiences and they in turn 'could read anything they liked into her'.

There have been other show business stories; that Vivien Leigh did not cost as much as an established film star and therefore this was an added attraction. When

David Selznick had to buy Clark Gable for the rôle of Rhett Butler from his father-in-law, Louis B Mayer of Metro Goldwyn Mayer, it is estimated that it cost him nearly £1,000,000 in the end.

But Director Cukor denies this. 'In a film costing 3,750,000 dollars whether Scarlett was paid a little more or less would not have mattered at all. It was the type we were looking for.'

In fact Vivien Leigh was paid 15,000 dollars which by 1938 Hollywood standards was what a young film actress with her modest experience was worth.

Since she had first read *Gone With the Wind* a few years before, Vivien, like hundreds of other actresses, had wanted to play the part of Scarlett. Margaret Mitchell's best seller had rarely left her side but the chance of her even being considered was so remote that she dismissed the idea from her mind.

The self-imposed exile between Vivien and Larry, due to their work, was not working out. They missed each other terribly.

It was late autumn in 1938. Vivien had been offered a part in a revival of Tyrone Guthrie's *A Midsummer Night's Dream* and Olivier was in Hollywood where he was making *Wuthering Heights*. It was studio gossip that Olivier and his co-star Merle Oberon did not hit it off and his daily letters to Vivien were loaded with misery.

On the day a letter arrived at Durham Cottage from Olivier saying that he was on crutches due to a severe case of athlete's foot Vivien made up her mind. Even if it meant only five days with him in Hollywood it was worth the expense. She went straight off and booked a ticket on the *Queen Mary*.

At the back of her mind was also a slight hope that if

Merle Oberon dropped out of the film she could step in and take over the part of Cathy which she had wanted from the beginning. Instead she had been offered the subsidiary rôle of Isabella which Olivier had advised her to turn down. He insisted that with her experience now she must only go to Hollywood in a starring rôle and not as a supporting player.

Vivien kept very much to herself on the ship but was to be seen up on deck with her head buried in *Gone With the Wind*, day after day. It seemed that she was bent on soaking in every detail of Scarlett's tempestuous character, almost as if she had a premonition of what lay ahead.

Rested from the trip Vivien arrived in Hollywood and had never looked prettier. From her personal success in *The Mask of Virtue* she had acquired self-confidence and poise. Besides she was in love – as in love as any woman can be – and it showed in her face.

Vivien Leigh and Laurence Olivier were at the romantic peak of their lives. The conventions of marriage had not yet dimmed their physical and emotional awareness of each other. They were by any standards the most glamorous and decorative couple either side of the Atlantic.

Arriving in Hollywood, Vivien was immediately plunged into the *Gone With the Wind* holocaust. She could hardly have avoided it as the whole film colony was bemused by the antics of David Selznick and the search for the right Scarlett.

Laurence Olivier had asked his agent, Myron Selznick, David's brother, if there was any chance of Vivien trying for the part. Myron Selznick, who knew that the film had already started without a Scarlett and time was running short, suggested that Olivier bring her along to see the big exterior shot of the fire in Atlanta that was being shot the next night.

On a forty-acre lot at the back of the Culver City, dozens of used sets from the old Pathé studios had been dumped to represent the city that Sherman so ruthlessly destroyed before starting to march to the sea. In a single night £5000 worth of junk timber soaked in kerosene went up in flames and all the Selznick executives had gathered to watch this great exciting shot.

It was just after midnight when Vivien took her place against the rail on the platform that George Cukor and David Selznick had erected for themselves.

The whole sky became lit up as the flames raged. Olivier looked at Vivien with her hair blowing in the breeze, her face lit with the glow and eyes flashing with excitement.

'Just look at Vivien tonight,' he said to Myron Selznick. 'If David does not fall for her I'll be surprised.'

During a lull in the fire David Selznick came over to shake hands with Olivier and be introduced to Vivien. 'David,' said Myron, 'I'd like you to meet Scarlett O'Hara.'

It was said as a joke that could have fallen embarrassingly flat. David Selznick just nodded curtly and went back to his fire. It was not until they were all having a drink in David Selznick's office early in the morning that he turned to Vivien and asked if she was interested in Scarlett.

Vivien's smile told the answer.

'All right, then you'd better have a word with George here.'

Recalling the occasion George Cukor says: 'I remember my office was nearby where I had these endless test scenes. I gave her one and said quite simply "read it". She read it in a piping English voice and I was rather rude and funny about it.'

Apart from her voice which could be altered once it acquired a Southern accent, George Cukor liked her unsentimental approach and she looked like Scarlett. She had the

Paul Popper

Miss Leigh (*above*) with a friend, Mr Jack Merivale, at the wedding reception of her chauffeur, shortly after Sir Laurence Olivier's marriage to Joan Plowright. (*Left*) Miss Leigh with her mother (centre), Mrs Gertrude Hartley, and with her daughter Mrs Suzanne Farrington.

Camera Press

The end of a marriage.

same well-bred, arrogant beauty with a touch of the hell-cat that few men could resist.

Next morning Cukor told David Selznick that if something could be done about Vivien's voice she was a probable candidate.

Back at the Beverly Hills hotel, Vivien slept very little of what was left of the night. She and Laurence Olivier went over and over the possibilities of her getting the part and its implication. She had not been too pleased with her own reading of the part, but Olivier was sure that no woman had ever looked more like Scarlett O'Hara and was backing his own hunch that she would get the part.

The next day came the photographic test. There was little time for too much preparation and no time to attempt a southern dialect . . . this was to come later.

One scene chosen was the one when she dresses in her bedroom before the barbecue. The shot shows her Negro mammy pulling hard on the corset laces with Scarlett urging her on 'tighter and tighter'. The other was when Scarlett tells the reluctant Ashley that she loves him and therefore he must love her.

Leslie Howard was a tremendous favourite on the set. He was a seasoned actor who knew his craft and his opinion carried weight, although he confessed he had never read the book.

After the test Howard told Vivien that he had liked the way she had handled the part. She had given it just the right amount of arrogance that Scarlett would have used. Cukor promised to let Vivien know the results.

Somehow she and Laurence Olivier lived through these days of suspense. By now he had made some friends with whom Vivien was able to spend her time. Most days Olivier was on the set of *Wuthering Heights* where he and Merle Oberon had patched up their differences.

The day that Vivien was supposed to leave to return to England and begin rehearsals for *A Midsummer Night's Dream* she made up her mind that she would give it just three more days. She cabled Tyrone Guthrie for extended leave and followed it up with a pleading letter. Few people could resist Vivien, and Guthrie, though anxious to begin rehearsals, cabled back that if such a major decision was in the balance he would wait.

Vivien was just beginning to give up final hope when Cukor phoned to say that the studio wanted yet another test, this time to see whether in fact her slightly prim English voice could be taught a Southern accent in so short a time.

Still the delay went on. During this time there were endless conferences between Selznick, Cukor and others near the heart of the film. It was a chance, a long chance, to cast an English girl in such a plum, obviously American, rôle.

There was another factor to be taken into account, too. The vast American, puritanical matriarchal society had to be considered.

How could the studio publicity department gloss over the fact that Vivien had left her husband and child and was living with Laurence Olivier? Hollywood liked its newcomers to conform to the book of rules as it already had plenty of trouble on its hands with many of the big stars who led untidy domestic lives.

Christmas morning 1938 came. Hollywood was bursting with egg-nogg and mint-julep parties. George Cukor held one of the most lavish and gregarious ones in his home in Beverly Hills and naturally Vivien and Laurence Olivier were asked.

By now Vivien had given up all hope though Laurence Olivier was not so pessimistic. She merely treated it as farewell fun before the agony of parting to go back to England. Practically all the chosen cast of *Gone With the Wind* had been invited. Vivien and Larry arrived late and Cukor soon sought her out. They stood drinking in the garden when with perfect timing he steered her off until they were alone and said: 'Oh, by the way, we have made our choice.'

Vivien, with her impeccable manners, braced herself so that she would not embarrass him by showing any disappointment, when he quietly said: 'I guess we are stuck with you.'

The Film of a Lifetime

WITH SCARLETT O'HARA finally chosen David Selznick was all ready to announce the news to the world. Although Olivia de Havilland and Leslie Howard had been cast for their rôles as Melanie and Ashley some weeks earlier, the news had not yet been released. Selznick wanted the full impact of publicity by giving the Press all the names together.

On 13th January 1939, in front of the studio's cameras and the Press, Vivien Leigh, Olivia de Havilland and Leslie Howard signed their contracts. Vivien already looked the part with her hair parted in the centre, clipped severely down at the ears and puffing into loose curls. She wore a simple dress and her lucky lion and unicorn brooch.

The first two weeks of filming were the happiest of the entire six months. Cukor was a sensitive woman's director. In explaining why in fact he was dropped from the film after only two weeks, some writers claim that Gable found him too sympathetic to the ladies.

But looking back today George Cukor disagrees. 'It is nonsense to say that I was giving too much attention to Vivien and Olivia. It is the text that dictates where the emphasis should go and the director does not do it. Clark Gable did not have a great deal of confidence in himself as an actor although he was a great screen personality and maybe he thought that I did not understand that.

'My own theory after all these years is that for David Selznick *Gone With the Wind* was the supreme effort of his career and it so happened that everyone who started with this picture never finished it. He was enormously nervous about the whole thing.

'I had worked on the picture for a year and shot for two weeks, some of which is still in the film. It was a great trial but also David Selznick's undoing, and he did things that he had never done before. For the first time he wanted to come down on the set and watch me direct something that we had worked out together. It was very nerve-racking because in the end a director has only got to satisfy himself.

'We never had any real break but maybe Selznick lost his confidence.'

When the news bush-fired through the studio that Selznick had replaced Cukor as the director, Vivien and Olivia de Havilland were rehearsing the big charity ball scene. They immediately looked at each other and ran off the set down the long corridors clutching their crinolines.

'We were both desperate,' Vivien said. 'We couldn't believe that it was true as George had worked out the whole conception of the characters for us. We loved every minute that he was directing us.'

'We were both crying and we must have argued with Selznick for an hour. I can see him now backing away from us into the window seat behind his desk. But he wouldn't give in. He had decided that Victor Fleming, a former camera man and Gable's favourite director, should take over.'

Looking back on *Gone With the Wind* now, Olivia de Havilland says: 'George Cukor has a marvellously intricate imagination which works on a very fine scale. Take a look at the scene where Mammy's lacing up Scarlett – it's just crammed with tiny, fleeting expressions and motives – and then at the next one when Scarlett sits on the stairs eating a chicken leg. There is no other scene in the film with so much detail, such richness – those were Cukor scenes.'

Hollywood writer Charles Samuels has his version in his biography of Clark Gable. 'Gable objected to George Cukor. Cukor was a woman's director and Gable was afraid that Cukor would throw the big scenes to the actress playing Scarlett, which would submerge his rôle. Selznick assured Clark Gable that if he thought his rôle had become secondary after the film was shot, everything possible would be done to remedy it.'

There were also script difficulties. Gable objected to the script when on hearing of Scarlett's miscarriage he was supposed to break down and weep. He could not reconcile the character of Rhett Butler crying over any woman and in any case he personally thought that there was nothing more contemptible in a man than self pity. He simply could not bring himself to play the part this way.

In the end the scene was shot both ways and Clark Gable, always a gentleman and hard-core professional, admitted that Selznick had in fact been right.

Meanwhile Vivien was getting all the practice she could at perfecting a Southern accent. Will Price, Maureen O'Hara's husband, was called in to tone her down as at first she made the mistake of overplaying it to a point of being unconvincing.

'Once it was decided upon, I discovered that there was no joking about playing Scarlett. From then on I was swept along as though by some powerful wave,' Vivien commented when recalling the film some years later. 'It was Scarlett, Scarlett, Scarlett night and day, month after month.

'Perhaps if I had struggled, wished and worried about getting the rôle I might have been afraid. As it was I had no time to let worry get the upper hand. I lived Scarlett for close to six months from early morning till late at night. I tried to make every move, every gesture true to Scarlett and I had to feel that even the despicable things Scarlett did were my doing.

'Scarlett fascinated me but she needed a good healthy old-fashioned spanking on a number of occasions and I should have been delighted to give it to her. But she had courage and determination and that is why women must secretly admire her – even though we can't feel happy about her too many shortcomings.'

They were long, exhausting days for Vivien with few intimate friends to share her worries. She was pushing her strength to its very limit and used to cry herself to sleep many a night. She frequently had to pull herself up from snapping at some small irritation.

The cast found her friendly although even then, as in later years, she rarely mixed with them off set. People thrown together in a touring play or film tend to become one small intricate world of their own. But Vivien always maintained a certain aloofness and kept to herself in her time off.

The job of keeping Vivien sweet was given to Clark Gable.

'Vivien Leigh and Clark Gable were quite polite to each other, but I don't think for one minute that they were specially interested. They were good chemistry on the picture, that's all. I never heard her talk of him off the set,' says Cukor.

Charles Samuels, an observer of those *Gone With the Wind* days, tells an interesting incident which took place at the end of the film.

'The two stars got along well until the picture was finished. But one morning they were called to MGM to make advertising stills. The call was for eleven in the morning. Clark was on time but not Vivien Leigh.

' "Where's the star?" Gable asked Larry Barbier who was in charge.

'Barbier said that he would find out. He had followed the usual procedure of sending written notes to both stars the day before asking them to be on hand, costumed and made up by 11 am sharp.

'The gate policeman said that Miss Leigh had not yet arrived. This would mean considerable delay while she was being dressed and made up.

' "I did not know what to do," said Barbier. "Clark was a man who could overlook almost anything but having you lie to him. But I knew that if I told the truth he wouldn't wait, so I took a chance. I didn't want to lose him as long as I had him there.

' "She's being made up right now," I said, hoping that Leigh would arrive in the next few moments and be almost ready before Clark started to get restless again.

'And he was pretty patient. He waited for another half hour then came storming out of his dressing room. "What the hell is this?" he demanded. "You told me she was in make-up. If she was, she would be here by now, wouldn't she?"

' "Yes," Barbier said, and explained that he had lied and why. Gable thought that over, then asked:

' "Did you put the call through for her yesterday?"

'Larry said he had.

' "In writing?"

' "Yes."

' "Time and Gable wait for no actress," he told Larry, and left.

'That was shortly after twelve.

'Vivien Leigh arrived at one o'clock.

'A few days later another appointment was made for taking the advertising stills. This time both stars were on time and were apparently once more on excellent terms with each other.'

In addition to being on the set twelve or fifteen hours a day, six days a week, Vivien had the added strain of being in a different country, speaking in a different accent from her own and spending hours in intense heat and dust. Studio publicity told how twenty tons of bricks had been pulverised to simulate the red dust of Georgia. Scarlett spent long days shooting in this stifling air.

Most days Vivien was at the studio at 6.30, had her breakfast while having her hair done and then was made up. By 8.45, word perfect, she was on the set ready to begin the day's work. The cast seldom left till nine or ten at night.

Because of the many changes in writers – eleven in all – who worked on the film, the cast found it difficult to keep track of the nuances in the character they were playing. Vivien had her own way of dealing with this. She always kept Margaret Mitchell's book at hand and, when a scene came up that she found had changed in its conception since it was originally written, she rushed to her dressing room and quickly read the original text in the book. This gave her a sense of continuity which was necessary for her own acting sanity.

Whenever Vivien felt that vital dialect from the book was being overlooked she would protest to Selznick.

One day when everyone's nerves were stretched and the heat was particularly trying Selznick caught her altering a line and bawled her out in front of the cast:

'Put that goddam book away and concentrate on the film I'm making.'

It is an interesting thought what would have happened if in fact Vivien Leigh had been allowed to complete the film under George Cukor's direction. There is no doubt that the rapport between these two people was sensitive and strong and probably Vivien would have given a deeper and more subtle interpretation of Scarlett had Cukor handled her.

As it was she would go over every Sunday to Cukor's house and discuss what scenes lay ahead.

'It was probably terribly irregular but I couldn't have finished it without him.'

After a few weeks she found out that unbeknown to her Olivia de Havilland was doing the same thing. Whenever she got confused she would telephone Cukor for a little bit of black-market direction.

Six weeks after he had started Victor Fleming was almost a nervous wreck and was replaced by yet another director, Sam Wood. Later when Fleming recovered he went back on the film but in the end was so disenchanted with the result that he would not accept his Oscar or attend the première.

All through this panic Cukor kept the two girls sane. Says Cukor: 'Naturally Vivien was a good friend of mine and when she was sulking or worried about something then I would give her some advice. I don't think it was great coaching but I did work with her on the whole part. She knew that I knew it and I also knew her.'

On one occasion when Vivien was in a bad temper on the set she demanded:

'Let's go down and look at the last scene and then maybe we can get some idea of it.'

Vivien used to go over to the Cukor house for lunch on Sundays. She was so exhausted that after a swim she would fall asleep by the pool.

'As the sun went down we would just cover her up and let her stay there. She used to delight in giving an impersonation of me telling her how to do some sort of a love scene. I would be using four letter words to get something very primitive and shocking in her. The part of Scarlett has a very earthy, primitive, tough side and a kind of ruthlessness that was in contradiction to her looks and delicacy. Vivien's impersonations were terribly funny with a very bogus American accent.'

Had the film been made later in Vivien Leigh's career she would have been much more exacting and demanding than she was. Considering that she had the most exhausting rôle of anyone in the film she showed few bursts of temperament and even these were due in the main to her desperate physical tiredness. This sense of disciplining herself never left her throughout her career.

One of the chief difficulties was the erratic way in which the film was shot. Unlike playing in the theatre, where an actress is allowed to develop her rôle in a natural sequence, Vivien found herself often with little preparation being asked to play three scenes covering a gap of six years on three different locations all in one day.

This switching on and off of various moods and ages is trying for really experienced actresses, let alone a relative newcomer.

'This was the hardest part of all for me,' Vivien said. 'Sometimes we were only given our lines for the following day late at night and I never seemed to know more than twenty-four hours ahead even what age I would be playing next day.'

There were many great scenes in *Gone With the Wind* which made cinematic history. But the shot that did more than anything towards Vivien Leigh winning her first Oscar was the scene when Scarlett falls on her knees in the fields at Tara and vows that never in her life again will she go hungry.

This is how it was made. One night, after working at the

studios until eleven o'clock, the camera crew, director and Vivien moved out into the country to capture that emotional scene shot against the sunrise in the ravaged fields of Tara.

To make it as comfortable as possible for Vivien, who was showing strain and fatigue, a trailer was set up as a dressing room near the scene. There all dressed and made-up she waited until 2 am.

By the time that the dawn did show up Vivien was so tired, so desperately tired and angry as the shot was repeated time and time again, that she finally fell on her knees in a fury and beat the earth. It was magnificent. No amount of training could have captured her wild fury.

All the way back to town in the director's car she sulked with rage. Next day she sent a note asking the director to come to her dressing room. There and then she apologised for her behaviour. A small thing perhaps but it is a typical gesture of Vivien Leigh.

All film making is tedious but *Gone With the Wind* because of its six months' duration seemed an eternity to the stars playing in it. Even so there was time for some fun. There is one magnificent shot where Rhett Butler takes Scarlett in his arms and carries her up that long, long staircase to bed. After it had been done twelve times the director said:

'Let's try it just once more, Clark.'

Gable grimaced but picked up Scarlett and began the long climb once more, every muscle aching.

'Thanks, Clark,' said Fleming. 'I really didn't need that shot . . . I just had a little bet on that you couldn't make it.' Gable took it magnificently.

Vivien Leigh always said that her most exhausting scene was the one when Scarlett struggles through the streets jammed with people evacuating Atlanta. It took all day to get a few feet in the can and every time there was a pause the make-up man had to rush out and wash off some of the grime to give the right shade of dust from the Georgia clay.

In a mass spectacle like this the part that the public does not realise is the difficulty that the actors and actresses have in getting themselves physically to the right spot at exactly the right moment for the cameras. Often it has to be so accurate that a small stone or cross on the street marks the spot.

For Vivien it not only meant being in full charge of her acting emotions, and registering all the horror of the scene, but she had to see that she coincided in split-second timing with the stampede of horses and carriages.

'I can assure you that it is not a pleasant experience to see a gun caisson charging down on you – even when you know the riders are experts,' she said afterwards.

'In fact I was so intent on being in the right place at the right time that I did not realise until I got into bed that night how battered and bruised Scarlett O'Hara had become.'

Vivien claimed that her greatest acting challenge was the scene when Scarlett shoots the deserter.

'I remember that after that nerve-racking episode both Olivia de Havilland, the wonderful Melanie of the film, and myself were on the verge of hysterics. The memory of the realistic dead man's fall down the staircase was to live with us both for a long time afterwards.'

The last weeks of filming had become almost a nightmare for Vivien. How she kept up her strength is a tribute to her own professional attitude to work. She never missed a day's shooting.

During the last few weeks David Selznick met her in the corridor and truthfully, but tactlessly, he said:

'My God you look old.'

'And so would you if you had been working eighteen

77

hours a day for weeks on end,' she snapped back.

The opening shot of the film had been filmed in December 1938, where Scarlett cries to the Tarleton twins: 'Fiddle-de-dee! There isn't going to be any war, and I'm tired of hearing about it.'

But in the perverse ways of Hollywood at the end of filming in August, Selznick wanted the scene re-shot with Scarlett wearing a white dress instead of the flowered green one she wore at the barbecue. Telling Vivien this he took one look at the tired, strained girl in front of him and told her to go away and have a six weeks' holiday before re-shooting the scene.

'He was right. I looked like an old hag and felt even worse,' said Vivien.

Although Scarlett gained Vivien Leigh an Oscar and made an international film star of her, able to decide on her own scripts and fees, she never liked the part.

'I knew it was a marvellous part, but I never cared for Scarlett. I couldn't find anything of myself in her, except for one sentence. The odd thing is that they would cut it out in the various re-writing that went on, but I always fought to have it put back. It was the only thing in the character that I could take hold of. It's in the scene after Frank's funeral when Scarlett gets drunk and tells Rhett how glad she is that her mother is dead and can't see her.

' "She brought me up to be kind and thoughtful and ladylike, just like her, and I've been such a disappointment." I liked her then for her honesty.'

War

IT WAS SEPTEMBER 1939. Letters from friends in England were unsettling and the tension of Europe had stretched across to California which was recovering from a sun-baked summer. The small British colony around the Ronald Colmans tended to cling together speculating on the future and gathering comfort from exchanging scraps of news from Home.

The first weekend in September was Labour weekend when the studios would be closed for three whole days. Douglas Fairbanks, Junior, already a confirmed Anglophile, arranged for a party of friends to rendezvous at Catalina Island, a pleasure resort off the coast of Catalina.

Recalling the weekend, David Niven says that the Fairbanks hired a yacht, and Nigel Bruce was a fellow guest as well as Vivien Leigh and Laurence Olivier. The Colmans and other friends were taking over their own boats and meeting up at the island.

On 3rd September, everyone on the Fairbanks' yacht was up early to hear the news on deck. The sea was calm and the sun already warm by 8 am. They gathered round the radio as Neville Chamberlain's measured voice came through: 'This country is at war with Germany.'

'We were all completely stunned for a minute. There was absolute silence as the radio was switched off.'

Vivien Leigh stood with tears sliding down her cheeks. Slowly the various couples disappeared to their own cabins with their own thoughts. Her concern was for her daughter Suzanne, her parents and young Tarquin Olivier.

How could they be brought to safety?

'After a while,' says Niven, 'we had all collected ourselves and began to drift back. Douglas Fairbanks broke the tension by appearing with a bottle of champagne and glasses.

'I remember we all drank a toast to victory and then I put on my water skis and dinner-jacket and went overboard.'

David Niven was to spend six-and-a-half years in active service and was, in fact, the first volunteer from California.

For the rest of the weekend there was little else to do but sit around and talk. At that moment of isolation they all felt completely helpless and the men decided to report to the British Embassy on the Tuesday morning.

On Tuesday it was back to the studios for Vivien where she was fretfully finishing re-takes for *Gone With the Wind*. It all seemed so inconsequential now that war had been declared. Olivier's orders from the British Embassy had been to stay in Hollywood, and his situation would be reviewed again when he had finished his present film commitment in *Rebecca*.

Plans for the launching of *Gone With the Wind* were already under way. The film had been finally cut and edited and shown to a select private audience. Selznick was overwhelmed – it was evident that they had created a masterpiece. Viewing the film in its entirety, all the pettiness, frustration and gruelling work were forgotten. And through it all came the electric performances of Vivien Leigh and Clark Gable.

No one had doubted Gable's success in the rôle of Rhett Butler. The rôle and the script had been tailor-made to fit his cinema image and even if his mouthful of blazing white teeth were false and his ears did have to be stuck back, when he looked out of the screen into the dark cinema auditorium every woman present felt it a very private moment between herself and Gable.

But with Vivien it was different. She mesmerised every member of that audience not only by her beauty and strength of character but a magic that filled the screen. Here was a great film star and everyone knew it. Selznick had moist eyes when the lights went on.

The première in December was Hollywood at its most gigantic-stupendous. Olivia de Havilland, Vivien Leigh, Claudette Colbert and Laurence Olivier flew down to Atlantic City in one plane, and Carole Lombard and Clark Gable in another with a trailer-streamer proclaiming 'MGM's *Gone With the Wind*'. A State holiday had been declared and a five-day fiesta.

With a letter from her mother bearing the news of wartime preparations in London it seemed incongruous to Vivien as she boarded the plane in a shower of confetti. There was the première itself and a spectacular costume ball with Vivien as the centre-piece. From there on to New York to an even larger première as the film opened simultaneously at both the Astor and the Capitol. New York audiences were ecstatic over 'Scarlett' and following it all in England was the man who had advised her against doing the rôle – Alexander Korda.

Looking back over this period where Vivien Leigh had now been recognised as the 'hottest thing in pictures', George Cukor says she was so modest and touchingly child-like about Laurence Olivier.

'It was wonderful. Whenever you said anything to her she would say, "But of course, Larry is such a marvellous actor and he's a brilliant director. He knows everything," which of course at that time was not true. He became it later but not then. But Vivien's belief and faith in him were remarkable.'

After hearing her ramble on about Laurence Olivier one day, Fanny Brice, who was a very wise and amusing woman, said to Vivien, 'You sure are stuck on that guy, aren't you?'

In 1940, Hollywood made the great discovery of the Victorian novels and Jane Austen. As an antidote to the gangster-film period, women cinema patrons now revelled in seeing pretty films with froths of petticoats. Cashing in on the 'romantic era', Metro Goldwyn Mayer decided to make Jane Austen's *Pride and Prejudice* with George Cukor, already established as the top 'women's director', and a script by Aldous Huxley. Cukor had his characters well in mind when he asked for Vivien Leigh as Elizabeth Bennet, but once again the studios had other plans. Illtimed as it may have been, MGM was preparing a wartime 'weepy' called *Waterloo Bridge*, and had Vivien in mind as the unsophisticated little dancer and Robert Taylor as the toffee-nosed Scottish aristocrat. With the very real possibility that once again they would miss their chance to act together, Vivien implored George Cukor to try and persuade the studios to accept Joan Crawford in her place as the dancer as this would free her to play Elizabeth Bennet. In the end it was a toss-up between the gentle Greer Garson, then new to Hollywood, and Vivien, but MGM were convinced that the public would not overnight accept 'Scarlett' as 'Elizabeth' and the part went to Greer Garson. Vivien was landed with *Waterloo Bridge* and Robert Taylor.

Waterloo Bridge was an unashamed 'women's film'. There wasn't a dry handkerchief in the cinemas, either side of the Atlantic, where it packed in the patriots. Vivien, as the out of work dancer who, with disarming insouciance, defies the wartime posters to 'go into factories' and becomes a prostitute instead, was pale, frail and touching. The curious clothes of the period only emphasised her snowflake fragility. Her performance was so appealing that the girls of Half Moon Street instantly moved their business over to Waterloo Bridge, which later became a 'must' on every American serviceman's agenda.

The film demanded very little of Vivien and was almost a holiday after the intensity of *Gone With the Wind*. In off the set periods she used to closet herself in her dressing room with Dame May Whitty. There was a strictly 'no admittance' air, but passers-by could hear Dame May putting Vivien through scenes from Shakespeare.

Although Vivien's voice had developed considerably since her *Mask of Virtue* days and was right for films, it still tended to be reedy and lacked the carrying power and resonance demanded by Shakespeare. On the set of *Pride and Prejudice*, Olivier was seen to be more preoccupied than usual. He rarely mixed with the rest of the cast and the rumour began, 'Olivier is on to something'.

At nights and weekends the gregarious 'Oliviers' (as Hollywood called them, despite the fact that they were not yet married), were no longer available for parties. Only Danny Kaye, who lived next door, and a few intimate friends knew the reason. They were planning to invest their entire savings in a production of *Romeo and Juliet* on Broadway.

The fact that frenzied New York audiences may not have been ready for *Romeo and Juliet*, or Shakespeare, never entered their heads. They were ready – it fitted their mood. For the first time they would be able to act together and with one of the classic love stories of all time they felt they couldn't go wrong.

But they did – tragically.

The Bingo Marriage

THERE SURELY HAS never been a more bewitching Juliet than Vivien Leigh or aggressively healthy Romeo as Laurence Olivier. Vivien's black-haired wigs only emphasised the magnolia pallor of her skin and her slight figure made Juliet's tender age seem believable. Olivier, though perhaps too old in years for Romeo, had a feeling of unleashed passion in his flanks.

All the sets and costumes were devised in England by Elizabeth Montgomery and Peggy Harris who, as the firm of Motleys, produced some fresh and inspiring ideas. With a £24,000 budget, of which £12,000 was Vivien Leigh's and Laurence Olivier's own money, twenty-one scenes were prepared on the old Vitagraph studio. Oliver, in his rôle as director, was inspired by energy, and divided his time between rehearsing his cast and dashing out to the studios with some new inspiration.

Vivien adored the rich and luxurious clothes she was to wear. Dame May Whitty had been persuaded to play the rôle of the nurse and Alexander Knox, from the Old Vic's early days, Friar Laurence and Edmond O'Brien Mercutio. Vivien's own difficulty was in the lyrical passages where she had to sustain her voice for long periods. She found the balcony scene with its tender flowing cadence particularly difficult. With her basic instinct of being honest with herself she realised that she lacked the acting experience of projecting the subtle details that Shakespeare's girl-bride demanded.

Romeo and Juliet opened in San Francisco with two very

84

insecure and exhausted people wondering how they would be received by the critics in their first big theatrical adventure together.

Vivien was terribly nervous on the first night, but this only brought a quality of youth to her performance. Olivier, who enjoyed telling the story against himself in later years, had the kind of ghastly experience every actor dreads. Came the moment when Romeo vaults over the wall of the Capulet garden. In the leaping, Olivier misjudged his strength and was left suspended from the balcony like a puppet. The incident was the more noticeable after his bouncy performance throughout the rest of the play. One Chicago critic was later to rename the play '*Jumpeo and Juliet*'.

In Chicago the company opened to a vulgar display of publicity. Advertising trailers in the cinemas announced 'Come and see the Great Lovers in Person'. Their arrival at Union Station had all the excitement of a Beatles send-off today. The play itself underwent a critical reappraisal and tightening up. More money was poured in and nothing spared for the spectacular New York opening.

Two important factors that influenced the play's reception in New York were whether in fact this was the right time to try a Shakespearean love story, with the phoney war in Europe entering its second more serious phase, and, even more important, the built-in resistance by the serious theatre critics to film stars from Hollywood attempting classical acting. The fresh New York publicity, 'See real Lovers make love in public', could not have helped either.

All the friends were there for the opening night in May 1940, along with the normal smart New York theatre set. Vivien had stocked up the Oliviers' hotel apartment with flowers and drinks for the customary after-the-show party. The box office reported healthy bookings indicating a long run. There were 'good luck' cables from England stuck up on Vivien's dressing room mirror. The intense excitement had brought a pallor to her cheeks.

'She looked incredibly sweet. She really looked like the virgin fourteen-year-old that Juliet was meant to be,' an American member of the audience now recalls. 'Olivier had that right amount of awkwardness but I do remember that he seemed to bounce about a lot like Douglas Fairbanks senior in his wild days, and we staid New Yorkers did not expect this from Shakespeare.'

The critics were merciless. 'The Worst Romeo Ever', was the temper of criticism. Vivien came in for her share, too. As Brooks Atkinson of the *New York Times* wrote, 'Let it be said in her favour that she makes an earnest attempt to act the part as it is written. But she is not yet accomplished enough as an actress to go deep into the heart of an imaginative character wrought out of sensuous poetry.'

Shattered and completely bewildered, somehow they both held their heads enough to face the appalling situation that the next day people were actually queueing outside the 51st Street theatre asking for their money back.

Olivier, more in anger than in sorrow, issued a statement that all tickets returned could have cash refunds. They moved out of their hotel rooms to a house on the West Shore that Katherine Cornell had lent them for weekends, and sent back all the drinks and 'goodies' they had intended to use on weekend friends.

When the play closed after twelve days they were both broke. They had lost their entire savings and their confidence had taken a terrific beating. During that week Noël Coward had invited them to a ball he was arranging in aid of war relief.

Vivien Leigh and Laurence Olivier were to be the star

attractions. Feeling despondent, and insecure, however, they both decided that they could not let Coward down and they must go. Vivien dressed up in the ball gown she had intended to wear and with fixed smiles they arrived to Noël Coward's: 'My darlings, how brave of you to come.'

After three years of waiting and secretive living, Vivien Leigh and Laurence Olivier at last heard on 28th August 1940 the news they had been waiting for. They were now both free to marry.

If either Jill Esmond or Leigh Holman had hoped for a reconciliation it was now apparent that this was useless and for everyone's sake there was no point in waiting any longer before divorce proceedings.

Horrified at the possibility of 'a typical Scarlett O'Hara wedding' in the vulgar Hollywood style, Olivier phoned Ronald Colman to seek his advice. Colman, who had managed his own wedding to Benita Hulme, adroitly suggested that instead of applying for the licence in Los Angeles, where every registrar's office boasted a newspaper stringer, it would be better to go just a hundred miles away to Santa Barbara, register with the local clerk who had no interest in movie people and return there after three days when they would be free to marry.

It was Benita Hulme who suggested the practical idea to marry in the small cottage on their ranch. Here they could at least hope for some privacy as both Olivier and Vivien desperately wanted their wedding to be something special and romantic that they would remember for the rest of their lives.

To avoid attracting attention, it was arranged that Benita should go to her own jeweller and say that she wished to add a gold ring to her present one but as Vivien's fingers were bigger, she would have to pretend that she wanted it a little larger.

The Colmans decided to go on ahead to their schooner, *Dragoon*, and wait there for the newly-weds when they would all go on a three-day honeymoon.

Before leaving for the ranch the Oliviers gave a small party to their friends and though bursting to spill their news it is fascinating that not one person present there suspected anything, not even when Vivien and Larry wished everyone the best of luck when they said goodbye.

The local judge had agreed to perform the marriage at one minute past twelve on 30th August when the necessary three days would be up. Standing under the warm sky in full moonlight and facing east towards England the judge proceeded. He had warned the couple that he would keep it short.

The Oliviers' marriage must be one of the quickest in history. After one quick 'yes' from Vivien he pronounced the couple man and wife and then ended up with the exclamation, 'Bingo!'

Vivien never did hear the word bingo during the rest of her life without bursting out laughing.

Back at the schooner romantic-minded Benita Colman had transformed the one small cabin into the kind of bridal suite that even Scarlet O'Hara would have enjoyed – lace-edged pillows and masses of Vivien's favourite white flowers.

At 3 am the newly-weds finally arrived driven in the Colmans' car and went on board to join their hosts in the smallest possible wedding reception. There were just the four of them with a small white wedding cake and champagne. Skipper Colman took charge and very soon they were all heading for Catalina Island. Vivien and Laurence Olivier stayed up on deck leaning over the prow of the ship as they sailed into the dawn and a new chapter in their lives.

Next morning they swam and sunbathed and speculated whether the news had leaked out in the gossip columns of Hollywood. The news did not in fact break till late that evening.

For Vivien Leigh her new status as a recognised wife meant even more than the wedding had to Olivier. Women are more sensitive to the nuances of living irregularly and Vivien hated the deception of the last three years especially as unsophisticated Americans were not as tolerant as the permissive society of Shaftesbury Avenue.

Vivien Leigh had three wedding rings during her marriage to Laurence Olivier. The first one given her in the Californian ceremony was lost sitting in a cinema watching *Les Enfants du Paradis*. Olivier then gave her another ring which was chased and which she wore all the time.

'But I really wanted a plain gold one so he gave me a third ring inscribed, "This is the last one you'll get. I hope." '

This Vivien Leigh kept locked up in her jewel box – in case she lost it.

A Persian Kitten

IT WAS Sir Alexander Korda who found the solution of how best to use the Oliviers' talent now that war had been declared. With the flop of *Romeo and Juliet* on Broadway, which had meant the loss of their combined savings, and the anxiety about their respective children in England there seemed little point in remaining in the pampered isolationism of America. But on the instructions of a close friend, Lord Norwich, then Mr Duff Cooper, the Oliviers were advised to remain there until it was decided how they could best be used in the war effort.

While Vivien fretted and wrote long encouraging letters back to all their friends, Laurence Olivier resumed the flying lessons that he had begun several years before with the London Aero Club.

George Cukor recalls how Vivien would come to fill in the hours at his house, swimming or talking and reading by the pool.

'Every time a plane went overhead no matter how large, Vivien would loyally insist: "There goes Larry." '

Both the Oliviers were now deeply involved in reading every book available about Nelson and Emma Hamilton. It was while they were living in New York at Sneden Landing, the house Katharine Cornell had lent them, that the telephone had rung with an excited Alexander Korda on the line from Hollywood. In his engaging, fractured English he asked them if they were prepared to come to Hollywood and make this patriotic film.

For the Oliviers it was a miracle – first the chance to

make a film together and the immense relief in being able to consolidate their finances again. For Vivien especially Alexander Korda had a touch of magic about him. This cultivated Hungarian had taught her so much about the good things of life – food, wine, art and people. She adored him.

The story of Nelson and his Emma was tailormade for the glamorous Oliviers and, even if history was bent a little in favour of Lady Hamilton, no one minded. The film was a low-budget one made in six weeks and though it did little to consolidate Vivien's ability as an actress she always maintained that it was one of the happiest films of her life.

Lady Hamilton or *That Hamilton Woman* as it was titled in America was the expected box-office hit and became not only Sir Winston Churchill's favourite film but through this Vivien was acclaimed the darling of the Russian Army. Even today she remains a top favourite and Russians outside Moscow are firmly convinced that in fact she is Russian.

A copy of the film was always kept at Chartwell:

'My father used to show it in the private cinema whenever we had important guests until we, the family, all knew it by heart,' says Sarah Churchill, Lady Audley. 'He never tired of seeing it and it was through this film and his admiration for the Oliviers that they later became friends.'

With the film finished, money in the bank, her daughter Suzanne and mother Mrs Gertrude Hartley safely arrived from London and living in Vancouver, Vivien was free to return to England.

Three days before Christmas 1940, on their last day in Hollywood, the Oliviers invited a few friends to say a casual goodbye.

'They were living in a rather melancholy house that

91

had been built by Dorothy Parker in a canyon,' says George Cukor. 'Dorothy used to say, "There descends on the house in the late afternoon what I would call a suicide light". It was a rainy Sunday and everything was packed and standing in the hall. Dame May Whitty and her husband were among the friends. Then the moment came to say goodbye. Vivien beckoned me away, took me in the other room and threw her arms around me and began sobbing. She clung to me . . . She was such a good, good friend. Even today I am moved when I think about it.

'There was something about her, even when she was at her gayest and you would talk on the phone with her, in that lovely little voice, that touched one's heart. But this farewell was something I will never forget.'

Vivien's friendship with Cukor, also Hungarian, and now a grey-haired 'senior statesman' of the Hollywood colony, never faltered from the day they first met. He was probably her closest friend in America and the day before she died Vivien sent him a loving birthday cable.

Back in London the Oliviers experienced their first taste of wartime bombing. Exhausted, exhilarated and profoundly happy they both went to bed on their first night in London at Durham Cottage fully dressed. Vivien even wore her gloves.

During the next few weeks Vivien Leigh, famous film star, acclimatised herself to being the domesticated wife of Acting Sub-Lieutenant (A) Olivier, RNVR. Complete with their cat, Tissy, and her little old car, like any other young service wife she followed her husband from station to station.

In the beginning it was fun but Vivien Leigh has never enjoyed time on her hands. She became easily bored, irritable and then desperately depressed. Laurence Olivier was the first to notice the signs.

Together they looked for a play that would be a suitable vehicle for her return to the West End, this time as an established actress. She had already refused to go back to America to play with Cedric Hardwicke in *Caesar and Cleopatra*, saying:

'I am not going to let any film offers from Hollywood or plays on Broadway attract me away from my own country. My place is here beside Larry.'

It was Laurence Olivier who first saw the possibilities in the part of Jennifer Dubedat in Shaw's *The Doctor's Dilemma*. Vivien had seen the Katharine Cornell production in America and though she was not keen on the part the thought of wearing the flamboyant Edwardian fashions fascinated her. H M Tennent Ltd had agreed to put on the play and promised a lush production as an antidote to wartime anxiety.

Every morning, in their cottage at Warsash, Vivien and Laurence Olivier got up at 6.30 am and after a scrambled breakfast he went to his air station and she to the train. If the days were long and exhausting it never showed on Vivien for this was precisely the kind of challenge and excitement that suited her temperament. She was always in better health when she was occupied for eighteen hours a day and had always managed on little sleep.

Few people, if any, recognised the pale-faced girl with raincoat and head scarf as she curled up in a corner seat of the dimly lit train on the way home each night. With her head deep in Dickens she read her way through his entire works during the run of the play. Yet this was the film star whom Hollywood would have paid any price to lure back to their side of the Atlantic.

The play opened in the provinces and toured for six months before coming to London. The *Manchester Guardian* noted: 'Miss Leigh comes to the part with a good many initial advantages and played the earlier scenes with a quiet beauty and simplicity which she would do well to substitute for her mannered treatment of the last scene.' The *Manchester Evening News* was even more critical and wrote: 'Vivien Leigh has been wise in her choice but her cinema self obscures much of the cleverness of Shaw.' When the play finally reached the Haymarket it settled down to a record thirteen months' run with Vivien looking incredibly beautiful and outliving four leading men – Cyril Cusack, Cusack's understudy who played for a few nights, Peter Glenville, who went down with jaundice and finally John Gielgud who took over with four days' rehearsal.

By now the Oliviers had moved to a cottage at Denham where everybody converged at the weekends and the parties were hilarious. The John Mills were nearby neighbours.

David Niven remembers arriving there with Brendan Bracken, then Minister of Information. As he opened the door, 'there was Larry in some sort of rug singing the Messiah – that was something appalling – Vivien was draped in some extraordinary garment like a sheet and Bobbie Helpmann wore a leopard-skin jock strap with a kitten in it.'

Vivien Leigh was godmother to David Niven's eldest son, David. For his christening present she gave him a handsome Georgian drinking mug with the initials of his name David William Graham Niven. But somewhere the engraved initials had gone wrong and appeared on the mug as DWGW. From then onwards Vivien always called David Niven senior, 'Wivern'.

Vivien Leigh's personal friendship with George Bernard Shaw has been grossly exaggerated, but they did have a prolific postcard correspondence. When in 1943 the plans were being made for Gabriel Pascal's film of *Caesar and Cleopatra*, Shaw had naturally the final choice in choosing the cast. Gabriel Pascal wanted Vivien as the kittenish Cleopatra so Hugh Beaumont arranged the meeting between the author and Vivien. With great tact and intuition of the conceited and difficult Shaw, Vivien won his heart immediately. She took the only course possible by turning a most important moment in her career into amusing drawing-room talk. She never once mentioned Cleopatra. Shaw was completely aware that she wanted desperately to play the part and that Pascal wanted her to but he kept her in suspense until they said goodbye.

Looking into her pretty face he said: 'You look just like a Persian kitten and that is how I want my Cleopatra.'

With three months on her hands until the film began Vivien decided to join Hugh ('Binkie') Beaumont's Spring Party he was organising for ENSA to take to North Africa. The talent was pretty impressive with Beatrice Lillie, Dorothy Dickson and Leslie Henson. Everyone had musical comedy training, and could sing or dance, except Vivien. It is now odd to reflect that at the preliminary meeting at H M Tennent's, John Gielgud and the rest of the cast racked their brains trying to find out what in fact Vivien could do. It was agreed that her looks were enough but there had to be some excuse to get her on the stage.

Finally she had two spots in the show, one in each half, as well as appearing in sketches.

In the years between nobody quite remembers who suggested it first but it was decided that 'Sagittarius', the comic writer, should turn out a nonsense lyric, *I'm not such a scarlet Scarlett O'Hara*.

A Desert Rat who remembers her recalls today: 'It was like a miracle after the day's heat and dirt to see this absolutely divine creature in her long dress and picture hat. It didn't matter that we scarcely heard a word but she looked like peaches and cream.'

Afterwards the troops used to queue at the 'stage-door' to get autographs of the stars. Miss Dorothy Dickson remembers Vivien saying to her: 'Oh, Dottie, you have so much personality in your signature and mine is so drab.' Dorothy Dickson had first seen Vivien when lunching in London with Adele Astaire. 'Have you ever seen anything like that face?' Fred Astaire's sister had commented.

Another piece from Vivien's limited repertoire that went down well with the men was her recitation of Lewis Carroll's *You are old, Father William*. Tired, homesick soldiers sat spellbound in impromptu open-air theatres as this fragile wisp of a woman took them back to their childhood. Even at her most sophisticated in latter years Vivien Leigh always retained the mannerisms of an eager child. It was most endearing.

Sometimes a soldier used to arrive at the stage-door with some small present he had managed to buy. Dorothy Dickson remembers the night she received a box of chocolates which was considered a very rare treat. She was on-stage performing when she heard a scream from the impromptu dressing room she shared with Vivien Leigh. On coming off she was met by a terrified Vivien who explained that she had left the room for a second and when she returned 'a rat the size of a rabbit had jumped out'. To while away the time the two actresses used to play Scrabble together.

The concert party were given star treatment all the way as the guests of Generals Eisenhower, Doolittle and Spaatz. In Tripoli, where eight thousand troops saw the show in a great stone auditorium, General Montgomery entertained them afterwards. In Tunis on the terrace of

Paul Popper

A major milestone in the career of Sir Laurence. In 1956 he received for his work on the film *Richard III* the British Film Academy awards for the best film from any source, the best British film and the best British actor. The evening was even more memorable because Lady Olivier was chosen to present the awards.

Vivien Leigh was never happier than when surrounded by people, particularly celebrities. She is seen (*above*) with Sir Laurence and Noël Coward in a photograph taken by Tony Armstrong-Jones, now Lord Snowdon. In 1956 Marilyn Monroe arrived with her husband, Arthur Miller, to appear with Sir Laurence in *The Prince and the Showgirl*. They are seen (*left*) at London Airport. In 1964 Vivien Leigh made the acquaintance of Beatle Ringo Starr (*below*, *left*) with whom she travelled to the United States where she was to make the film *Ship of Fools*.

Air Marshal Cunningham's villa they gave a special moonlight performance to King George VI and eighty select guests. In talking to Vivien Leigh afterwards the King suggested that she should recite his favourite poem, *The White Cliffs of Dover* by Alice Duer Miller, but as it was the end of the tour she did not take up his suggestion.

By the end of the tour everyone was exhausted. In the mornings they had visited hospitals and convalescent homes and gave performances in the scorching sun of the afternoon and again in the evening. All the company lost weight and Vivien shed a stone, but they all felt desperately sad the day they had to return to England.

Back home Vivien started work in Pascal's *Caesar and Cleopatra* at Denham six days after the Normandy invasion had begun. When Pascal first planned to do the film in 1938 he was asked whether he was interested in using Vivien Leigh. He was not. It was not until six years later and she was again suggested that he thought she was right for the part.

It was an unhappy film for Vivien. 'She and Pascal were never on the same wave length,' says Jack Hillyard, cameraman on the film. 'Pascal was Hungarian and temperamental and all the cast found him difficult to work with.'

For the Oliviers this was personally a tremendously happy period. Laurence Olivier had just completed his stupendous Henry V and they were living in Old Prestwick, a charming country home near Prestwick. At the weekends Vivien continued to fill the house with friends. Angela Baddeley remembers:

'Larry brought back some of the spirited horses he used in Ireland in the Henry V film. On one weekend there was John Mills, Robert Helpmann and Stewart Grainger. They all eyed their fiery steeds with some mistrust.'

Angela Baddeley was thrown but mounted again and was able to ride home. It was not till she tripped on the stage of the play she was in several nights later that she realised that she had strained a muscle in her fall from the horse.

Guests arriving for the weekend were often met at the station by Laurence Olivier complete with cart and Blaunche Kyng, his grey gelding from Henry V.

Much to their absolute delight the Oliviers were going to have a baby. The fact that she was pregnant did not deter Vivien as she felt in her confident way that she could manage to complete the film before it was necessary for her to retire to the country. Sadly six weeks later she had a miscarriage and lost the baby.

Shaw made innumerable alterations to the script during the making of the film. For instance he sent Vivien Leigh a card: 'Your Claudius Caesar (Claude Rains) is not thin an d stringy (I have just seen him); so will you say instead: "You are hundreds of years old; but you have a nice voice etcetera." I think this is the only personal remark that needs altering; but if there is anything else let me know – GBS.'

Shaw had a rigid rule that not one word of dialogue should be altered in any of his productions without his consent.

The film took nine months to make and the budget soared from £500,000 to well over £1,000,000.

'Imagine how I felt in those thin costumes in the middle of winter starting at 8 am,' Vivien said afterwards and though she loved dressing up the intense cold soon began to tell on her. Soon after finishing the film she became ill. Since a child she had suffered from a weak chest. She was ordered to bed.

Her doctors forbade her to get up and attend the première.

But the critics enjoyed her. 'Of royal vindictive, cattish, cruel queenliness,' wrote one critic.

This was the best possible medicine she could hear.

Of all the modern rôles that she played Vivien Leigh herself preferred Sabina in Thornton Wilder's *The Skin of our Teeth*. Perhaps it was that in the mischievous minx Sabina she saw herself – the eternal woman.

Even the preliminary skirmish with her boss in Hollywood leading up to the production amused and excited her. She thrived on dangerous situations. Technically Vivien was still under contract to David Selznick but she had refused, at first gently and later outrageously, to return to America and make another film. It was 1945 and all through the war years despite a five-year contract she had managed to remain in England and be near Laurence Olivier. On the faintest suggestion that she owed Selznick any loyalty for his faith in starring her as Scarlett O'Hara, Vivien used to widen those shimmering green eyes and reply archly:

'Larry is playing in the most important part of all, that of serving our country, and I must be with him.' Besides there was another valid reason why she wanted to remain in England – to play Sabina.

All through her career Vivien Leigh had a compulsive urge to try something different and to those carping critics who after her death indicated that her acting ability was limited there is only one answer. Which other actress in modern theatre history has ranged from Shakespeare and Shaw to Tennessee Williams, Coward, Wilder and Girandoux with such facile perspicacity?

From the moment she read Wilder's modern morality play, *The Skin of our Teeth*, Vivien knew that Sabina was a part for her. She was not the faintest bit deterred that the witty Tallulah Bankhead had scored such a success in New

99

York and that the play might be baffling to staid British audiences. It was up to her to put it across.

In April, one week after the film *Caesar and Cleopatra* came to an end, the Oliviers went into hush-hush rehearsals at the Globe for H M Tennent's with *The Skin of our Teeth*. An irate Selznick sent a cryptic cable to Vivien Leigh that under his 1939 agreement he had plans to use her in Hollywood and when Vivien stubbornly refused Selznick sought legally to restrain her from appearing in *The Skin of our Teeth*.

With Sir Walter Monckton, KC, acting for Selznick and Sir Valentine Holmes, KC, for Vivien Leigh, the case was highly entertaining. During rehearsals the Oliviers were kept informed of the battle of wits between these two eminent lawyers. Sir Valentine won the case on the grounds that if Vivien Leigh was forced by an injunction not to act she ran the risk of being drafted by the Ministry of Labour into the Services or munitions factory. And clearly nobody wanted this. It was a brilliant legal sleight of hand and Selznick lost his case.

The Skin of our Teeth is the story of an average American family at grips with life. As Wilder explains: 'The Antrobuses have survived, fire, flood, pestilence, the seven-year locusts, the ice age, the black pox and the double feature, a dozen wars and as many depressions. . . . Alternately bewitched, befuddled and becalmed, they are the stuff of which heroes are made – heroes and buffoons. They are the true offspring of Adam and Eve. . . . They have survived a thousand calamities by the skin of their teeth.'

The rehearsals under Olivier had much of the loonery of the Marx Brothers' films. Every day new bits of 'business' would spontaneously evolve as the actors scrambled their way through the unorthodox structure of the play. Vivien played the rôle of the eternal serving girl, bathing belle and camp follower. In a shoulder-length red wig and a steady supply of black nylon tights which she had sent over from America for the beauty queen scene, she looked part witch, part woman and completely adorable. For balancing the girl guide goodness to Vivien Leigh's character was a turbulent, self-mocking, untamed streak. The two actresses who most influenced her life were Marie Tempest and unconsciously the majestic Mrs Patrick Campbell. From the former she learnt the axiom, 'Men are hell between the ages of forty-five and seventy,' and from the latter, 'Every great actress has a bit of the slut in her.'

The Skin of our Teeth opened at Newcastle where one thousand people queued from 7 am. It moved to Coventry where it completely baffled the audience and arrived in London at the Phoenix just ten days after the war had ended in Europe.

There was a special enchantment about the opening night. All Vivien's friends turned up in force, as much in curiosity as loyalty. Women, starved of glamour during five bleak war years, dived into their wardrobes and found forlorn evening dresses which they dolled up and wore. If there was a suspicious smell of moth balls among the gentlemen at the crush bar it was fully justified. Never before, or probably since, was that personal magnetism of the Oliviers more evident. And the play? – Wildly irreverent, stylish, curiously witty – an exhilarating antidote to wartime intellectual apathy. London went wild and fell hopelessly in love with Sabina. To every woman sitting in that audience Vivien Leigh was everything she yearned to be. And to every man she was the mistress that life had cruelly denied him.

On reflection Beverley Baxter's writing in the *Evening Standard* next day was not only a valid appreciation of the play but an analysis of the magic of Vivien Leigh.

'Miss Vivien Leigh is startlingly good. Forget about her Scarlett O'Hara, and her stiff performance of the artist's wife in *The Doctor's Dilemma*. We see her as she really is – part gamine, part woman, a comedienne, an artist.'

In the *Sunday Chronicle*, Beverley Nichols summed up her performance adroitly:

'Vivien Leigh gives a performance as sparkling as a diamond.'

Notley

'THERE IS NO glamour in being an actor . . . no glamour at all when you get to know him,' Laurence Olivier once said.

This was purely a personal opinion because to the thousands of British theatre patrons by 1947 the Oliviers were now indisputably established as the first family of the theatre. They were a romantic and glamorous couple, Laurence Olivier with his volatile strong features and Vivien Leigh who radiated a special excitement. Their very presence could lift a drab party into champagne heights, and they were both enormous fun to be with.

Iris Ashley Vowden tells of a breakfast party in Paris with the Oliviers and friends. They had nipped over to Paris for a weekend with Noël Coward and the John Mills. On the Monday morning Iris Ashley, then a fashion writer and old friend of Vivien Leigh, was asked to breakfast in their hotel.

'Everyone looked terrible. They had been late for nights. Larry was still in bed and looked ghastly. We all had breakfast in the Oliviers' bedroom and there was Vivien, looking fresh and simply marvellous in a silk dressing gown cut like a man's, pouring out the coffee. Somehow they all got to the station and I went with them as I was returning to London. I'll never forget Vivien in complete charge marching down the platform issuing orders to the porters right and left while the others all dragged behind.'

It was then that Noël Coward made the remark: 'She

has a body like swansdown and the constitution of a GI on leave.'

The first hint that Laurence Olivier had that he was to receive a knighthood was when a letter from the Prime Minister was delivered to him on the set of *Hamlet* at Denham studios. His first thought was to rush to the phone and call Vivien Leigh who was in Paris being fitted for her wardrobe for *Anna Karenina*. But he decided the call must wait till the evening.

The story goes that when he did finally track down Vivien and told her, she answered prissily: 'You won't take it, of course.' To which he replied, 'Of course not.'

For the investiture on 8th July 1947 at Buckingham Palace, Vivien with her instinctive good manners decided to underplay herself. She chose a simple black New Look two-piece, off-the-face hat and no jewellery. All eyes of the London crowds pressed against the rails outside the Palace were on Olivier with his golden mop of hair that he had bleached for *Hamlet*. Statistics have been given that there had until then been only nineteen other actors knighted since 1895 when Irving was called to Windsor by Queen Victoria. Their close friend, Ralph Richardson, had received his knighthood in the New Year's honours.

There are people today who say that Vivien Leigh enjoyed the indulgence of a title and even after her divorce from Sir Laurence Olivier she rigorously maintained her privileged status. This may be so, but it seems much more likely that though fully aware of the snob value of a title, especially in America, for sheer sentiment she wanted to retain her former husband's name. She enjoyed being Vivien, Lady Olivier.

While Olivier was completing *Hamlet*, Vivien Leigh made the film *Anna Karenina*. She always said afterwards that this was one of the few real mistakes in her career.

The reason may have been that there was no love lost between Vivien Leigh and another leading lady member of the cast. One day when everyone had been waiting around and tempers were frayed the other actress talked to the French director in French. Vivien felt it was affected and stood it for some time before retorting: 'All right, dear, we've all been to school and we all speak French.'

Much of the time Mrs Hartley spent on the set with her daughter, but when she was not there Vivien was always to be found sitting alone in a corner reading or doing the crossword puzzle from *The Times*.

Character actress Madge Brindley who had known Vivien Leigh for many years (she had first met Laurence Olivier when he was in Birmingham Repertory as a boy) speaks of the immense thoughtfulness of Vivien to her during this edgy film.

On one occasion Miss Brindley had asked if she could finish promptly at five o'clock as she had to get from Pinewood to London for a very important film test for Sir Alexander Korda. When five o'clock came and there was no sign of the director releasing Madge Brindley from the set she began to get nervous. She kept asking what the time was and looking flustered because every minute wasted on the set meant she might miss Korda, who did not like to be kept waiting. Noticing the unrest Vivien Leigh leaned across and said: 'What's the matter, Madge?'

Vivien Leigh listened to her story and said: 'Right, and the director knew about it and won't let you go now.'

Slowly and deliberately Vivien Leigh got up from her chair, walked off the set and collected her book and things lying on a nearby chair.

'We haven't finished yet,' the director called to her.

'Oh yes we have,' she replied coolly and walked off the set.

Next day when the same thing happened the director asked Vivien Leigh what was going on.

'If you let Madge go then I will stay,' the star replied.

Madge Brindley, who later in her career appeared with Vivien Leigh in the London stage production of *A Streetcar Named Desire*, recalls the last night Vivien was in the show.

'We all went to her dressing room for champagne before the second half. I was detailed to stand in the wings instead of a dresser and catch Vivien as she made a spectacular fall.

'There I was and suddenly I saw a white shroud pass over my head and heard a crash. I looked round and Vivien had landed in an armchair. I was terrified.

'She picked herself up and said quietly, "What happened, Madge?"

'I explained I didn't see her and she laughed and said: "I put a little drop of brandy in your champagne, dear!"'

It is these infinite attentions to other people that makes Vivien Leigh so unforgettable.

With all the drive, imagination and sincere make-believe of the theatre Sir Laurence and Lady Olivier made their new estate Notley Abbey into the ancestral home they never had.

It was a setting in grand style for the theatre royals of the postwar world. What the Barrymores and Lunts of America began in stylish living, the Oliviers completed. For the last ten years at Notley, when the household was running in full swing, they set a pattern in the theatre world which will not be repeated. After years of wartime austerity in dressing and eating the time was right to stretch back into the opulent thirties. And this Vivien, Lady Olivier, did with panache. At their height the Oliviers were larger than life itself and because of it they invited criticism among those who were not invited to share it.

After their nomadic war years spent both in Britain and America it was a natural reaction to want roots of their own. Mentally and physically they were both ready to settle down in a place of their own.

Vivien Leigh has enjoyed her own possessions round her (she always travelled with several paintings which she hung in hotel rooms round the world). But now they both felt that the time had come to have a permanent home in the English countryside.

During the years they lived at Notley it was like one vast set from a Terence Rattigan play.

'It was the last age of elegance and nobody in the theatre today has the time, energy or money to live on that scale,' Lady Redgrave, actress Rachel Kempson, said. 'Vivien made every weekend so special and wonderful. She was such a loving and giving person.'

Notley Abbey on the outskirts of the town of Aylesbury in Buckinghamshire, was founded as an abbey before 1160 by Walter Giffer, Duke of Buckingham, as a convent for Augustine monks. At the dissolution of the monasteries it had passed into private hands and for several hundreds of years belonged to one family.

It was a bitterly cold day in 1943 when the Oliviers drove through the painted white gates on the Aylesbury road and up the long tree-lined drive. They were both inwardly excited yet apprehensive of yet another disappointment. They had looked at so many houses.

Vivien Leigh was overjoyed when they crossed a small bridge over the gentle river Thame. She had a deep-seated conviction that she could never be happy unless she lived near water. She carried this belief to such an extent that her last country house, Tickeridge Mill, was in fact surrounded by water.

The car swung round the last part of the drive and pulled up at the thick oak front door. In grey stone with mullioned windows this noble house still has many of the character-istics of an abbey even though it had been used as a farm-house over the last hundred years.

Before the war and in the early part it had been occupied by a lady with a large family of children who had given it life and vivacity and a well-lived in air of dilapidation. But the Oliviers were seeing it under different circumstances. It was cold, damp, overgrown and melancholy.

For Sir Laurence it was love at first sight. It had romance, history and a presence. Vivien followed him as he stalked through the dark rooms and up the staircase in the central tower. For all her wild, romantic nature she had a fierce streak of common sense and almost reverence for bodily comfort. She could see that it would take a long time to restore (wartime building permits were very strict) and even more important, a lot of money. Though she was a lavish spender all her life she hated to waste money on mundane necessities.

For Sir Laurence, Notley was history, roots, England. He walked through the rooms like a man in a trance. When he heard that Notley had been endowed by Henry V (he had just completed making the film) he felt that this was a direct and private omen.

'Well, that's it,' he said firmly.

'That's not it,' Vivien countered.

Though by no means a flamboyant sentimentalist, Laurence Olivier has a very deep and real appreciation of the English historical scene. One cannot imagine him escaping to America or Switzerland for tax reasons or taking up any nationality other than British.

When they left Notley he had made up his mind. That night when they returned to London Vivien telephoned their close friend Robert Helpmann.

'Do come and see it and talk him out of it.'

Sybil, Lady Colefax, the interior decorator, and David Niven, who was in town, were also cajoled into giving their advice, and to go and have a look.

Everyone was a bit gloomy and pessimistic and talked about the primitive plumbing and the one small heater. Says Niven today:

'It looked absolutely hopeless.'

Laurence Olivier had an argument. If the place could be made to pay some of its way then everyone would be happy. There was enough land, seventy-five acres, to do a little farming and market gardening. He talked with irresistible charm and boyish enthusiasm. Such problems as damp and no heating were overshadowed by the sheer delight of breeding pigs and growing cabbages. And Vivien could have greenhouses for all the house plants and flowers she was wild about buying.

Sentiment prevailed over sanity. With the money from the film *Henry V*, Notley was bought a few months before the end of the war and builders moved in immediately to look after the essential work. The Oliviers planned to do each room up as the permits and money became available and in the weekends they drove down to see how the work was progressing.

Vivien Leigh had been playing in *Skin of our Teeth* for a couple of months and fellow actors began to notice how terribly thin she was becoming and how she tired easily. Once on the stage, the old trouper spirit triumphed, but the moment she came off she seemed to collapse with tiredness.

After friends began talking to her about it she finally

went to a doctor for a check up. He was alarmed and asked to speak to Olivier at once. He had diagnosed the first stages of tuberculosis.

'But Larry is in Hamburg' (where he was playing *Hamlet*), Vivien explained. 'It is terrible to worry him unnecessarily. Couldn't we have a second opinion before we contact him?'

The second doctor was more reassuring and said that some weeks in hospital with treatment and then a complete rest at Notley would be all that was necessary. There was no need to think of a sanatorium.

Vivien wrote to Olivier explaining this in a very un-alarming way but her letter never reached him. Instead he got a second note from her saying, 'Now you know the worst,' but did not enlarge on it.

Olivier was frantic with worry and lack of real news and at the same time he was unable to leave his production to come and see for himself. Finally he left Germany and arrived in Paris where their good friends, the Alfred Lunts from America, were staying. They had recently seen Vivien and were able to reassure him that all she had was 'a patch on the lung which is not considered serious these days'.

At the end of the month Vivien Leigh went into University College Hospital for six weeks' treatment before going to Notley to convalesce.

A nurse who took care of her at the time remembers: 'We were all so sad the day she left. It was like something going out of our lives. She always looked so glamorous and was such fun to steal in and have a gossip with. She knew all our names and by the time she left knew all about our private lives, too. She used to long for the day she would leave for home and I remember teasing her and asking if we were not good enough for her.'

' "I will have everything that I want at Notley – as well as my husband," she answered.'

It is only when one lives in a house that the whole character of a building emerges and you begin to feel its soul. By now Vivien had begun to love Notley and the house had proved even more manageable than anyone had thought possible.

The dining room could seat twelve comfortably which was a convenient number as the house only had five guest rooms.

For their own bedroom Vivien chose an L-shaped room where she could lie in bed and look across the meadows to the river Thame. She spent her days reading and ploughed through all of Dickens, although he was never a favourite of hers, the sayings of Confucius, Montaigne's Essays, Balzac and so on. She was probably one of the best read actresses in the world and was completely catholic in her choice of literature.

When the spring weather came she got up a few hours each day and lay on the terrace basking in the sun and planning her future garden. Roses were to be the main theme. In the walled garden at the side of the house, with its view of the ancient dovecot that had once housed 1200 doves, she planned her rose garden.

During all the summers that they lived at Notley you could find Vivien out with a trug in her rose garden every morning picking off the heads of the dead roses. She loved and cherished every bush and much to the gardener's dismay was a prolific picker. White roses were her favourite flowers.

Laurence Olivier's brother and his wife moved into the cottage on the outskirts of the drive and Dick Olivier took over the farming and market gardening side.

For Vivien, Notley Abbey had the same charm as did

the Petite Trianon for Marie Antoinette. She frivolously christened all the cows after parts she had played. There was Cleopatra, Titania, Blanche, Miranda, Ophelia, Juliet. But there was no Scarlett. She refused to allow any cow to be called after the girl who brought her fame.

Weekends at Notley had something of a royal command about them. Guests were asked to foregather at Durham Cottage, the small Chelsea town house of the Oliviers.

'It was usually after the theatre on a Saturday night as we had mostly all been working,' says Lady Redgrave. 'There would be something small like delicious little sandwiches and drinks. We would then split up into cars and begin the hour-and-a-quarter drive to Thame. As most of us were pretty tired it was a very pleasant way of unwinding.

'Arriving at Notley at midnight out of the dark was marvellous. All the lights would be blazing, huge fires everywhere and masses of flowers.'

Vivien Leigh liked her guests to dress for dinner. 'It's so good for the servants,' she used to say in a Noël Coward-ish way. She had a clear-cut understanding with her staff and they were expected to be on duty the entire weekend. Though there were always crises of some sort it is a triumph to her ability as a hostess and employer that in fact she managed to keep any staff at all. They were expected to achieve, and did, the impossible.

Everyone would meet in the library for drinks and then proceed to a four- or five-course dinner. The food was always superb. Though she always said she was no cook this is probably not true. Vivien Leigh knew and understood how to plan her menus and had the same meticulous approach to running her household as the Duchess of Windsor.

ul Popper

Paul Popper

1951 Vivien Leigh and Sir
urence appeared at the
ndon Palladium in a lavish
arity show, part of it in
oute to the great comedian
d Field, who had just died.
e of the hits in the show
s the song *Triplets* per-
med (*above*) by Danny
ye, Vivien Leigh, and Sir
urence Olivier. After the
ow, Vivien Leigh and Sir
urence (*right*), in costume
another sketch, con-
atulated each other on
eir performance.

In 1952 Sir Laurence and Lady Olivier attended the Royal Film Performance at the Empire Theatre, Leicester Square (*above*), accompanied by Mr and Mrs John Mills. The film that year was Mario Lanza's *Because You're Mine*. In March 1953 the Oliviers returned from America after Miss Leigh had suffered a severe nervous breakdown. They are shown (*below*) leaving London Airport.

Her mimosa eggs, watercress soup, cold soufflés and lobster Newburgh were memorable, and any new recipes or cook books she heard of were jealously brought home to be discussed at great length with the current cook.

Lady Olivier herself chose the wines and through the years had acquired a considerable knowledge of a cellar. When dinner was finished about 1.30 am most of the guests yearned to go to their beds. But not Vivien. Dazzling, irrepressible and so incredibly beautiful, in the flowing chiffon dresses or trim evening pants that she loved to wear, she would insist they then took part in her word games or cards. It was as if she cherished every minute of her friends and was loth to let them out of her sight. She hated being alone at night.

'She never tired. It was incredible. Larry and the rest of us would quite obviously be dying on our feet, but not Vivien. She simply never looked or behaved as if she was tired,' says Lady Redgrave.

Off the library was a small 'butlers' pantry'. Before finally going to bed, no matter what hour, Lady Olivier always inspected each breakfast tray. They had to be perfect.

Leading from the kitchen was another small room lined with shelves of china she had collected on her travels. She loved beautiful china and much of it was in her favourite colour, white. Each tray had to be set with its individual china and strictly to her instructions down to the last pastel linen napkin embroidered with VLO.

Even after the war when food was terribly scarce, somehow Notley always had everything for its guests.

This kind of thoughtfulness is the sort that you expect and never get in 'the stately homes of England'. But here was a woman who often gave six performances in the theatre a week, whose health was never strong and who by most standards had little staff anyway.

Looking back on Notley, Peter Finch wrote in a woman's magazine:

'An attitude circulated that these weekend parties were in some way exclusive gatherings of a small and somewhat superior theatrical clique. It was never like that. Vivien adored her home and she was never happier than when she could share the peace and beauty of Notley.

'I think Larry would have appreciated their being on their own a little more. But Vivien was one of those people who must have people around her. They were not wild parties nor in any way particularly unusual—except possibly that they gave us a chance to relax and be ourselves far removed from the artificiality that surrounds much of life in the theatre.

'Larry, I remember, spent much of his time enjoying his hobby of tree pruning. I spent one glorious afternoon employed on nothing more glamorous than cleaning out a stretch of clogged-up river.'

A friend recalls a weekend she spent at Notley during the time she and Vivien played in *A Streetcar Named Desire*. Tarquin Olivier was home from school on a long weekend.

'Danny Kaye was also there and I remember he brought down a delicious cheese-cake. It was a very gay lunch and suddenly Larry took the cake and slapped it straight on his own face like in one of the old custard pie comedies. He was terribly funny and I think it was done for Tarquin's sake.

'I can't even remember whether in fact we had eaten any or not, but anyway Vivien always had so many delicious things it wouldn't have mattered. Larry and Danny were very funny, giving impersonations of people they knew and singing duets together.'

Just as the British Royal Family still likes playing charades at Balmoral and making their own entertainment, the Oliviers and their guests gave impromptu cabaret turns. Guests rarely got to bed before sunrise.

In the last sad days of Notley, when the Olivier marriage was under great strain, and Lady Olivier spent hours wandering round the deserted rooms while her guests slept, her passion for perfection never left her.

Somehow between playing in the theatre, planning productions, and leading a full social life in London she always found time to order just the right cheeses from that special shop, to see that the right new book was placed at the bedside of a guest who would enjoy it and to make each friend feel that this was one of the most cherished and special weekends of his or her life. It is a very special gift.

Unlike Sir Laurence, Lady Olivier bloomed when Notley was filled with guests each weekend. All his dreams of a weekend sanctuary, where he could plan and work on his big productions, faded as the car-loads arrived.

Vivien Leigh's choice of guests was catholic. And if they tended to be top names in their profession this was not through snobbism but merely that men and women who are experts in their professions tend to be more interesting.

Her theatre friends were legion – the Rex Harrisons, Redgraves, Lunts, Noël Coward, Terence Rattigan, Peter Finch, Danny Kaye. Because she was passionately fond of music, Sir Malcolm Sargent and oboist Leon Goossens were also great friends.

When Sir Laurence appeared tired or remote and took himself off to his 'workshop' or went out and pruned some trees Lady Olivier would airily comment: 'Larry is in one of his brown moods.'

He desperately needed rest. He needed peace to think. Perhaps this is where some of the trouble began in their marriage disenchantment. As each year went by Vivien Leigh depended on people more and more for stimulation and became more restless if she was alone. It was one of the symptoms of her illness.

Husband-and-Wife Team

THE OLIVIERS' TEN-MONTH tour of Australia and New Zealand in 1948 was a splendid and courageous undertaking. Partly sponsored by the British Council, it was the first time that a major English company had visited these enthusiastic, theatre-hungry countries.

It was not that Australia and New Zealand were ignorant of theatre – their own lively amateur repertory companies saw to that. But it was a question that up until now, apart from a few exceptions (D'Oyly Carte for instance), by the time an English Company had reached the Pacific, it had run through the stand-ins from the original company. Even if the principals might be passable the rest of the company were usually lamentable and subsidised by drawing on local talent.

The Oliviers were quite determined that this would not happen and the entire company would be up to standard. And it was. In addition to their theatrical status they had the added responsibility of being treated as unofficial representatives of Buckingham Palace.

The sea voyage out not only made it possible for the cast to rehearse, which they did in the dining room every morning before lunch and afternoon before tea-time, but gave them the chance of welding together as one family.

In the past the Oliviers have been criticised for choosing so many of their friends for their overseas companies. But this is a fairly natural reaction. A long tour is an unnatural situation and it is not only necessary to know a person's professional stamina but also his private behaviour and

117

temperament if the company is to be kept free of friction.

Few people outside the theatre realise the strain of physically moving half the world away a company of fifty people, their personal trappings and the tons of scenery involved. In addition there is the challenge of constantly adapting scenery into cinemas and opera houses of all shapes and sizes.

The final choice of plays fell to Olivier who settled on Shakespeare's *Richard III*, Sheridan's *The School for Scandal* and Thornton Wilder's *The Skin of our Teeth*. The Wilder play was a complete gamble and there are still bewildered people in Australia today who talk about 'that Marx Brothers' performance – what was it?' On the whole, entirely due to Vivien's twinkling performance as Sabina, the play got interesting notices.

The entire tone of a trip like this is set by its principals and Laurence Olivier and Vivien Leigh set the standard high.

'They were avidly interested in everything we did. Larry adopted a patriarchal attitude towards our behaviour in general and Vivien took a keen personal interest in birthdays, love affairs and so on', a member of the company recalls.

'Every birthday was remembered with small parties and presents. Vivien was a compulsive and generous shopper. On the way out she practically bought up the entire ship's shop of cashmere sweaters and perfume. She always seemed to know exactly what you would like and couldn't afford to buy for yourself, such as a pretty antique ring or just the right silk scarf to match something that she knew you already had.'

Although she had always declared in interviews that she loathed gossip, in fact Vivien Leigh adored it. 'She simply hated to feel that there was something going on in the company that she didn't know about. She tended to be jealous of any pretty girls in the company.'

Always fastidious about her clothes, Vivien Leigh's dresser with the company also acted as her personal maid. One of Vivien's super-fastidious quirks was that she liked every piece of her underwear to be wrapped in tissue paper. If fresh tissue was not possible then the old stuff had to be re-ironed until it was smooth and looked like new.

One morning her dresser was ironing her underwear in the wardrobe room screened off from part of the stage. Two of the boys of the company passing were most intrigued and decided to play a joke. They screwed up some tissue and fluffed up small breasts in a petticoat. The joke fell very flat. Miss Leigh was not amused.

When some of the younger members of the cast decided to 'live it up' in one of the Australian cities, Laurence Olivier called the whole cast together and said they were behaving 'like Aussies on leave in the war', and he would not stand for it.

One of the saddest moments of the tour was when Laurence Olivier received a letter that New Boy, Vivien's Siamese cat, had been run over. He had to break the news to her and she cried so much that no one thought she could make the evening performance. She did but her face swollen from crying was noticeable under her make-up. New, as he was known, was given this unusual name because 'he was new when we got him'. Vivian adored him and took him everywhere in an elegant Parisian collar ornamented with tiny gilt bells. She always took him on tour and he was completely at home in various hotels and theatre dressing rooms.

For the Oliviers the social side of the tour was even more strenuous than their work. Australia lionised them. They visited universities, factories, war memorials, theatre groups, besides the endless British Council receptions and official parties at the various Government Houses.

It was while visiting a glass-blowing factory in Sydney, where a troupe of players were presenting in the lunch hour Molière's *Le Malade Imaginaire*, that the Oliviers were to meet the leader, Peter Finch, who was to become a close personal friend.

After the performance, Olivier said to Finch, 'If ever you come to Britain, let me know – I'll do all I can for you.'

In New Zealand, the travelling pace was even greater. They covered over 1000 miles and gave forty-four performances in just under six weeks.

By now Vivien Leigh had not only become adept at making the little speeches required of her but actually seemed to enjoy them.

It was in Christchurch that Olivier's knee, which he had injured in Sydney, gave out. For several nights Vivien watched him apprehensively struggling on crutches until finally he had to give in. The doctors had only one suggestion – to remove the cartilage. The Oliviers discussed whether to wait until they returned to England before operating but this seemed impractical. With a heavy season at the Old Vic ahead of them, it seemed much more sensible to have the operation there and then, and use the return trip home by sea to recuperate.

Vivien Leigh, who had gone aboard the *Corinthic* the night before, was up on deck at 7 am next morning to watch Laurence Olivier being hoisted aboard in a canvas sling in the heavy rain.

While the rest of the company slept in their cabins, from high up on deck in her mackintosh, she stood out in the wind and rain to wave goodbye to the wet little group of fans on the wharf.

Back from that profitable tour with £40,000 in the kitty for the British Arts Council, the Oliviers began planning for a full season at the Old Vic. But no one, at least the principals, could foresee the upheaval on their immediate horizon. It was a bitter-sweet home-coming.

In Australia Laurence Olivier had received a letter from Lord Esher, chairman of the Old Vic, which had reached them in Sydney. It announced a change in the governing policy of the Old Vic. At the time there was very little Olivier could do about it but now that he was home a verbal confirmation from Lord Esher confirmed the decision. Laurence Olivier's services on the governing body, along with Ralph Richardson's and John Burrell's, would not be renewed after the present period of office terminated.

Shattered and bewildered Vivien Leigh and Laurence Olivier kept their opinions to themselves and a few trusted friends and threw themselves whole-heartedly into the new Old Vic season ahead.

Laurence Olivier intended to revive *Richard III* and add *The School for Scandal* as well as introducing the dramatic *Antigone* by Jean Anouilh. The rest on the ship had restored their nervous and physical energy and Laurence Olivier's knee was still painful but at least mobile due to the successful operation he had in New Zealand.

The situation was especially piquant because husband and wife would be appearing on the British stage together for the very first time.

From those early pre-marriage days, when they made the film *Lady Hamilton* with such success, Laurence Olivier had cherished the idea that as an acting team they would play in the theatre all the great classical rôles together.

Films were money spinners but he wanted Vivien Leigh to develop slowly into a powerful dramatic actress; besides, he thought the stage their natural *métier*. *Gone With the Wind* and its itinerant success had blocked this ambition, for although it made Vivien Leigh the most sought-after film actress in the world it took years for her to be accepted as a serious actress in the theatre world.

Though she longed to play *Antigone* – she always thrived on challenge – Vivien Leigh could not see herself in the part of the tinsel Lady Teazle. It took some persuasion from Laurence Olivier who delighted in this witty comedy and relished playing the part of Sir Peter.

In the eighteenth-century dress showing off her fragile waist, and the powdered wig her porcelain complexion, it is doubtful if there ever has been a more beguiling Lady Teazle. Whatever her private thoughts, with her usual professionalism she gave a performance which one critic dismissed as 'negatively perfect'.

It was thus in *The School for Scandal* that the Oliviers took their first curtain together. All night before, fans had slept on the pavement at St Martins Lane.

Recalling the opening a fan now says: 'There was a kind of magic in the air. It was not only the opening of a new season with them acting together for the first time, but somehow we all felt the excitement of having the Oliviers back. The Old Vic seasons were never the same without them. I suppose it was a kind of glamour that they gave off that we enjoyed.'

Some actresses are actors' actresses and others belong to the public. Vivien Leigh was the latter and the public adored her. She gave them everything. And professional troupers that they were, Vivien Leigh and Laurence Olivier accepted the responsibility of being the stars of the show. The rest of the company always takes its tone from the stars.

Laurence Olivier stopped to talk to the queue waiting patiently through the cold night. He joked with them and told them he hoped they wouldn't be disappointed. Vivien Leigh was more concerned with how they were being kept warm and if there were hot drinks available.

Even the rest of the cast and the stage hands felt the extra importance of the occasion. This was no ordinary first night.

As usual Vivien Leigh had transformed her dressing room into a salon. There was even a special corner for her new Persian kitten which Laurence Olivier had bought her to replace New Boy.

Every half hour more flowers would arrive from friends and fans.

Antigone was the second play of the season but in Vivien Leigh's mind it was one of the most important steps forward she had ever taken.

No one doubted that she would look superb, but would her voice have the tones and range required of this great dramatic rôle.

In the early years Vivien Leigh had studied voice production under Elsie Fogarty and taken singing lessons with Barardi but she and Laurence Olivier had worked together over the years on enlarging and enriching the range of her voice. Before every new season she always took a course on voice production.

'I used to have the worst voice in the world. Do you know what cured me? I had a voice teacher who told me never to wear high heels because they throw your body out of balance,' she explained.

It is interesting to digress that at the time of her death people who met Vivien Leigh for the first time invariably remarked on her soft husky voice. Whereas friends who had known her early in her acting career remember quite clearly when she spoke in 'a light piping voice'.

Her new voice virtuosity was to prove invaluable when

Vivien Leigh played Shaw's impertinent teenage Cleopatra and Shaw's sophisticated siren Queen of the Nile.

Antigone is the contemporary version of the Sophocles tragedy. It was first performed in Paris in 1942 when France was part of Hitler's Europe and dictators and storm troopers were part of everyday life. Though first performed in Athens in the fifth century BC the French found a parallel in their wartime occupation horror. They found strength and courage in Antigone's reiterated 'No!' to the King Creon. Oddly enough the unsubtle Germans allowed the play to be performed presumably because they found Creon's arguments for dictatorship in sympathy with their own.

The opening scene is set in Thebes. As the curtain draws backstage you see Antigone, her flowing dress and cape fall to the ground as she sits arms clasped round her knees. Her dark hair fits her head like a cap and her face is pale and taut.

The audience was electrified. Here was a new Vivien Leigh – powerful, emotional and authoritative. They were mesmerised as the Chorus (Laurence Olivier in evening dress) outlines the plot of the tragedy.

'That thin little creature sitting by herself, staring straight ahead, seeing nothing, is Antigone. She is thinking. She is thinking that the instant I finish telling you who's who and what's what in this play, she will burst forth as the tense, sallow, wilful girl whose family would never take her seriously and who is about to rise up alone against Creon, her uncle, the king.

'Another thing that she is thinking is this: she is going to die. Antigone is young. She would much rather live than die. But there is no help for it. When your name is Antigone, there is only one part you can play; and she will have to play hers through to the end.'

After the opening night performance, in January 1949, there was excitement in the foyer. As one member of that audience recalls: 'It was absolutely fascinating. The only thing people talked about was Vivien Leigh. This unbelievable sense of tragedy and nobility that she brought to the part. And her voice was so different. I remember one obviously regular theatregoer saying to his wife who sat next to me: "It is the first time I have thought she was a really great actress." '

As the play had relatively little movement in it, it also accentuated the perfect body control that Vivien Leigh had acquired. As a stage craftsman she showed that she had mastered how to breathe, walk, use her hands and feet and most of all her eyes. In addition she had that star quality that placed her as one apart.

'Streetcar'

THE PART OF Blanche du Bois in *A Streetcar Named Desire* and Sabina in *The Skin of our Teeth* were Vivien Leigh's favourite rôles.

Though in her private life she was distraught and nervous at the thought of ageing, oddly enough in her professional life she relished rôles that demanded that she not only look her age but that she should also destroy her beauty. She felt it was a challenge to her tormentors, who always insisted that her looks outweighed her acting ability. Besides one of her most endearing sides was that she was a kitten with fully-grown claws. And all these three parts required exactly this ingredient.

Vivien Leigh read *Streetcar* as far back as 1948 when it had its first initial success in America. With her built-in business antennae, and uncanny knowledge of what parts were right for her, she knew the rôle of Blanche du Bois suited her. From that day on she set her sights on being the first actress to play Blanche in Britain – and she never wavered.

At the time Hugh ('Binkie') Beaumont of H M Tennent was in America scouring for suitable plays for the West End. The night before he left New York he was told that the Broadway bush telephone was predicting that a play opening the following night in New Haven and written by the savage, unpredictable Southern playwright Tennessee Williams would be a winner. It was earthy, sensitive, box office and had a leading rôle that could give the actress playing it the chance of making theatrical history.

Beaumont himself did not wait to see the opening of *Streetcar* but told Irene Selznick (David Selznick's widow), who was handing the play, that he was interested and could Tennent's have first choice?

Overnight, just as it had been predicted, *Streetcar* was a sensation. Next day New York papers, stunned, shocked and mesmerised, were ablaze with the harsh brilliance of Tennessee Williams and his formula for a new kind of technique and excitement in the theatre.

Resting after *Antigone* in the Old Vic season, Vivien Leigh followed it all with quiet determination. By now the play was hot box office property and every theatrical 'angel' wanted it.

But Irene Selznick remembered her promise to Tennent's which, as the biggest theatrical agents in Britain, was the natural choice to handle the play. On arrival in London to place it, she called at Tennents office in Shaftesbury Avenue and a deal was completed in record time. A telephone call to Vivien Leigh telling her she had the part of Blanche put her mind at ease and Laurence Olivier was asked to direct. It couldn't have worked out better.

Two months after the 1949 Old Vic season finished the Aldwych theatre was secured for *Streetcar* and rehearsals began. Irene Selznick had reserved the right to represent Tennessee Williams' interests in seeing that the play was staged in London without too many alterations from the original American version.

On Broadway Elia Kazan, the 'method' director, had produced the play with the kind of truth and simplicity that Tennessee Williams wished and both he and Irene Selznick wanted the same feeling in London.

To authenticate the production the prompt script that Elia Kazan had used was lent to Laurence Olivier. Respectful of talent Olivier did automatically adopt many of Kazan's ideas but, in fact, on the London programme was written a credit line, 'After the New York Production'.

During rehearsals Kazan had come to London to produce *Death of a Salesman* and though the two producers tried on several occasions to meet they were unable to.

To add to the authenticity of the London production the set designed in New York by Jo Mielziner which Kazan had also worked on was used.

It was one of the most expensively produced plays in London, costing round £10,000. From the day of the first rehearsal there was a feeling of excitement about the production. As a fore-runner of the 'kitchen sink' era rumours of its erotic quality whipped up interest in the Press.

For Olivier, who was later to say 'the most painful undertaking of my career', *Streetcar* was more than a challenge in direction. It was a war between his conscience and admiration for the power of Tennessee Williams' script and a production that would be acceptable to London audiences.

For London in 1949 was far from ready for the shock tactics of this play. Vivien Leigh in her admiration for Tennessee Williams was blind to the fact that the play was idiomatically so paradoxical to the Southern States and therefore difficult to transplant. But it was Sir Laurence's job to make it tenable for reserved London audiences.

Typical of this was the fact that Olivier wanted to cut some lines from the play. He felt that they would be misconstrued as dirty by a London audience and this was far from the intention of the playwright. They are when Stella tried to vindicate to Blanche her love for Stanley.

'But there are things that happen between a man and a woman in the dark – that sort of make everything else seem – unimportant.'

Vivien Leigh argued and wanted them to stay in. Laurence Olivier wanted them out.

In the end it was suggested that the rehearsal continue and the matter would be resolved in the morning.

Next day a subdued and highly interested cast waited until this scene came up and found that in fact Olivier was prepared to go back on his former decision and leave the lines in.

Rehearsals were temperamental and exhausting. For Vivien it was a new challenge. 'Scarlett' was a spitfire kitten, 'Sabina' a beguiling tabby, but Blanche du Bois had all the subtleties of a thoroughbred Persian cat. Besides, the part demanded fantastic nerves and discipline. For two hours she was rarely off the stage and acting at high tension the entire time. It was the kind of challenge that she thoroughly enjoyed.

To know why Vivien Leigh gave such a great performance one must understand the fabric of Blanche's character and the motive of the play. Night after night, after an exhausting day of rehearsing, the Oliviers would sit up late thrashing out how the complicated and tragic rôle of Blanche should be played. Vivien always defended Blanche. She did not see her as a prostitute or nymphomaniac. She was a sensitive woman who through the shock of finding that she had married a homosexual, and perhaps being the cause of his committing suicide, had had her mind and values shattered. It was her loneliness that brought about her own decadence.

With this interpretation Vivien Leigh gave Blanche du Bois a poetic and dreamy beauty.

'I couldn't call it a drawing room comedy, but I am absolutely astonished that anyone should think it salacious,' she said, defending the play.

But as Laurence Olivier feared London was not yet ready

for such stark truth. As one critic wrote:

'I felt as if I had crawled through a garbage heap.'

To add to the realism of the part, for the first and last time in her acting career, Vivien Leigh even had her own dark hair dyed spun gold! She also had a wig made exactly like her own dark brown hair and wore this in daily life. As this was before wigs and hair pieces became accepted accessories in a woman's life, it was all the more amusing.

There were difficulties with the script, too. Some lines had already proved difficult in the Broadway production and were to be even more provocative in making the film. Compared with plays and films staged today, the text was mild but this was before the world accepted homosexuals, flower children, LSD and the Pill as normal school talk.

The whole key to the play is in scene six which takes place at 2 am in the sordid rented rooms of Blanche's sister and her husband in the Elysian Fields, a rundown area in New Orleans.

Blanche and her new friend, Mitch, have returned from the funfair. Mitch is depressed and carries a cheap plaster statue of Mae West which he has won at the shooting gallery. Blanche is tired and dejected with the complete exhaustion which only a neurasthenic sufferer can understand. The scene promises tenderness but with rapier finesse Tennessee Williams stabs his audience by turning it into the horrific crux to the play.

In the intimate blue light of early morning Blanche describes her first marriage.

'It was like you suddenly turned a blinding light on something that had always been half in shadows, that's how it struck the world for me. But I was unlucky. Deluded. There was something different about the boy, a nervousness, a softness and tenderness which wasn't like a man's, although he wasn't the least bit effeminate – still the thing was there.

'He came to me for help. I didn't know that. I didn't find out anything till after our marriage when he'd run away and come back and all I knew was I'd failed him in some mysterious way and wasn't able to give the help he needed and couldn't speak of!

'He was in the quicksands and clutching at me . . . but I wasn't holding him out, I was slipping in with him! I didn't know that. I didn't know anything except that I loved him unendurably. Then I found out in the worst of all possible ways. I came into a room and found my husband with an older man who had been his friend for years.'

It is then, and only then, does the audience realise the tragedy of Blanche and it is against this background that one must judge her craving for physical love and a respectable marriage.

Instead Tennessee Williams had her raped by her brother-in-law and spurned by the man she hoped to marry.

Throughout all the rehearsals Vivien Leigh listened but adamantly refused Irene Selznick's advice on how Blanche was played in America. She has always maintained that an actress must be given the right to interpret a rôle as she herself felt it and not blindly follow the author or director.

The result was a Blanche created by Vivien Leigh herself from the flutterings of her uncontrollable hands to the desperate nervous twitches of her head. It was the high-tension performance of a woman who herself knew mental illness and who fully understood the difficulties of the character she was playing.

In the final scene when the doctor and matron come to take Blanche away to the mental asylum she rose to dramatic heights that she had never attained before.

Bernard Braden, the young Canadian actor, who then played 'Mitch' in the London production of *A Streetcar Named Desire*, has a vivid impression of the first day the cast gathered for a read through.

'Vivien was wearing a black jersey dress and Renée Asherson, who played "Stella", remarked:

' "That's a pretty dress."

' "I'm glad you like it because you are going to see a lot of it," Vivian replied.'

And they did. She wore it every day until the show opened.

Braden had had an operation on the cartilage of his knee but because this was his great breakthrough in London he was anxious to conceal it from the Oliviers. In fact he was still using sticks but had purposely left them at home that day.

Vivien Leigh was the first to spot the limp, but when Laurence Olivier heard the cause they both went out of their way to make it possible for Braden to play the part with as little strain as possible. Olivier had had the same operation in New Zealand on the Old Vic tour and so in this way they were fellow sufferers.

Braden recalls:

'Vivien Leigh was not an instinctive actress. She was not an actress in the way that Laurence Olivier, who is probably the most successful instinctive actor in the world, is.

'Because she did not have this, Vivien had to work very hard and was conscious of the need for direction. She also became a perfectionist technically. For instance she could never interrupt a thought of her own on stage other than mechanically. She would always do it on precisely the same syllable whereas if the instinctive actress is playing the same part every night she will feel the need to change it.

'At the time it seemed slightly boring but it was not

132

until she was followed by another actress that I realised how much I had enjoyed Vivien's method. With Betty Ann Davies I never knew where she would be on the stage from one minute to another.'

One of Vivien Leigh's strongest points as an actress was her determination to improve herself all the time. This was not only in the case of the varied acting challenges that she accepted but, even once the production was underway, she went on working on it until the day she left the cast.

This was the case in *Streetcar*. At the time that Betty Ann Davies came in Laurence Olivier was appearing in *Venus Observed* and therefore unable to direct her. But Betty Ann insisted on a proper director and would not be broken in by the stage manager. Irene Selznick therefore arranged for an American director to come over.

Says Braden: 'I don't know what his brief was but he decided to redirect the entire play, not just Betty Ann Davies. And so it meant that for three or four weeks in July we were all rehearsing through the day in the new director's way and having to remember to play it with Vivien every night as Laurence Olivier had directed it. It became a little confusing.

'But the thing I remember about Vivien's reaction was that she said to me one night:

' "Is he injecting anything new and interesting into it because if he is let's try some of the ideas out on stage." She was only due to stay in the play for another three or four weeks but this was a mark of her willingness right up to the end.

'She was also a brilliant technician. If a light was six inches off its mark in a given scene I would not have noticed anything like that. But Vivien would. The moment she left the stage she would say to the stage manager: "Get that light fixed." She was able to perform and notice things and never missed a trick like that, not once.'

Vivien Leigh stayed in the play for eight months and Braden and Bonar Colleano for a further three.

'I would never stay in a play as long again but there was only one thing that used to make it possible for me,' says Braden. 'I had one scene with her when there was just the two of us on stage for about twenty-five minutes, and most of the time I was listening. She had one long, long speech where we sat side by side on a bench while she recounted to me a story. And after 200 performances I had heard that speech 200 times and it became boring. But as far as the audience was concerned I had to be hearing it for the first time. If I ever found myself getting bored to the extent that I sensed that the audience was noticing it, I could look at the line of her profile from her chin to her throat and at the end of that run I could get a lump in my throat. Just by concentrating on the sheer beauty of that line could bring me back to an awareness of her that I thought conveyed to the audience my interest in the speech she was giving.

'She was plastered with make-up. It was terribly over-done because of her dedication to the character of Blanche. She made every effort to destroy her own basic beauty in the way she made-up for this part. But as close as I was I could see right through that.

'It was incredible, absolutely incredible.

'Another indication to me between the instinctive actress and the non-instinctive one is that she tended to analyse everything. She always wanted to know why something worked and why something didn't work. In my view no one was more aware of her own limitations than she was – no one.

'I had to leave the production for two weeks when my father died. I had to go out to Vancouver and I got back on a Saturday afternoon, very tired, and I phoned the stage door during the matinée to say that I would be ready to go on on the Tuesday night as I had hoped to have the weekend to go through the lines again. I had a message that Miss Leigh had made a personal request that I would come and play that night. So I went.

'There is one scene in the play which is between Blanche, Stella and Stanley, and Mitch comes on at the very end merely to take her out. He arrives with flowers and she says:

' "Look who's coming! My Rosenkavalier! Bow to me first! Now present them." And he does an awkward, gauche little bow and she does a beautiful curtsey, accepts the flowers and the curtain comes down.

'That particular night as the curtain came down I turned to walk off stage and she said to me: "That's the reason that I wanted you to come back tonight as it is the first time we have had applause on that scene since you left." Now I was only in it for thirty seconds. We never got applause on that scene again, ever, because I immediately began to think what do I do in those thirty seconds that make it possible for the whole scene to get applause. And because I started to analyse it we never got applause again, ever. Presumably we had had it on every other performance up to then.

'I have heard her tear a strip off a prompter or stage manager but it is more difficult with fellow actors. And one night in the closing scene of the play, I don't know why, because it is a very fraught moment as she is led off, Bonar Colleano and I looked at each other and we both started to laugh – simply broke up. We completely killed the ending of the play, stone dead. And neither of us could have told why. Now this in my personal experience of the theatre can be a terribly dangerous thing because you've got to do it again the next night and you remember what happened before and it might happen again.

'What Bonar and I would have done between ourselves to solve that I don't know. It was a pretty chastening experience because we knew we had ruined the play. We were waiting for Vivien to blow up. What she did was to ask us to come to her dressing room and we had the sort of small-boys-at-school feeling. We went not knowing what was going to happen and all she did was to look up, smile at us and say:

' "That will never happen again will it?"

'And it never did.

'Which again was pretty skilful handling of a situation. There was no feeling of threat. I suspect that Vivien thought that Bonar and I were luckier than she was in that we were both instinctive actors and she wasn't. She was saying in effect to us: "It's all right for you two. You have it easy. But every performance is a job for me that I really have to work at and you think that you are more professional than I am because it is easier for you to act. So if you are really saying that you are that professional that will never happen again, will it, because I would never do it."

'She couldn't have said anything that would have a greater effect on us than that. If she had got angry we would have been very quiet and humble and then gone out and giggled with each other and might have done it again the next night.

'The thing about Vivien is that when I said she was not an instinctive actress that was because of rehearsing with her. But when I saw her from the other side of the footlights she fooled me every time. When I saw the film of *Streetcar* I couldn't believe it was the same woman. And I really didn't believe that she would stand up to Brando. I saw Brando play the part on Broadway and it was his play the whole way. But when I saw the film I thought she deserved every award she got. It was like seeing a different woman.

'Olivier did the play correctly for London audiences. I think if he had directed it for films in the States he would have probably done a very different production. This is where Vivien's mind comes into it. I think that she knew her own limitations and that Olivier knew her limitations. The difficult thing in rehearsals was that when he gave her a direction she thought was wrong, she was never certain whether it was wrong because he was missing a point in the play or because he knew that that was the only way she could play it.

'It wasn't till Robert Sherwood came over and saw the play in London and I met him afterwards that he said:

' "Well it is nice to have seen the play."

'And I said, "What are you talking about?"

'And he said, "This is a play about Blanche, this is what it is written to be.

' "In New York it was a play about Stanley because Brando was so strong. Now there is a balance in it and we have seen the play for the first time."

'And I began to reassess it then as I went through in performances and I came virtually to agree with him, although without under-rating Brando at all. Then when I saw the film I thought that Kazan had taken it a step further. Vivien, under Kazan's direction, had almost done the impossible. She had stolen the film from the powerful new idol Brando, even if they were both given Academy Awards for their performances.'

On the opening night at the Aldwych, Olivier refused to make a curtain speech.

'This is not my night. It belongs to my wife. It is hers alone,' is all he would say.

As a memento of the play Vivien Leigh gave Laurence

Olivier a golden Georgian locket with a strand of Blanche's spun gold hair inside.

Vivien never doubted that she was emotionally and physically strong enough to play the rôle night after night, but those around her were nervous. She had to be guarded against a nervous crash, not only for her own health, which at that time was very good, but for the London run which depended on her.

The fact that she played to a solidly booked out house for eight months without missing a performance amused Vivien Leigh immensely. Her only two concessions were that there would not be a Monday night performance and that all the ashtrays were to be taken out of the theatre so that the audience could not smoke, which upset her.

'It proves that I am not the hot house plant they think I am,' she said.

Both Tennessee Williams and Elia Kazan wanted Vivien Leigh for the film of *A Streetcar Named Desire* made in 1950. It was said at the time that Bette Davis and Olivia de Havilland would have liked to play Blanche. When it was known that Vivien herself wanted the part everything was settled. The rôle had already been tipped as a possible Oscar winner.

'I like rôles that I have played on the stage. I find that it does a great deal with my interpretation on the screen,' she said at the time.

Vivien and Elia Kazan, the new-wave American director, hardly knew each other and had only met a few times before. Prior to going on to Hollywood the Kazans asked her to stop off at their home in Connecticut so that they could discuss the part before filming and then travel across to Hollywood together. The rest of the cast who had been under Kazan in the stage production knew pretty well his working method and interpretation.

There were censorship difficulties, too, that were even more difficult than when producing the play. Somehow the scene where Blanche tells that her husband is a homosexual had to be played as realistically as possible and still get by the Hay's Office who were already nervous of the script.

As Elia Kazan recalls there were other problems for Vivien, too:

'She was up against something a little unusual in that she came into a company that had all played the play for a year and a half on the New York stage so that she was the outsider. She was the one who wasn't part of the unit. That takes time to overcome and she was a very proud person.

'The first three or four weeks were a little trying because I several times ran into her saying: "Well, when Larry and I did it in London," which gave me a pain in the neck. But gradually she and I got to know each other and she began to be more at ease with me and liked me I think as I certainly liked her. The references to how she and Larry had done it in England on stage stopped. I think she became much better because a stage performance is a different thing from a screen performance and the way she did it at first scaled to the stage seemed rather more artificial to me. By the time we got into the last weeks she was superb, I thought, and I think that in the last half of the performance in that film she was better than in the beginning.'

There were differences for the rest of the cast too. In the eighteen months they had been playing it on Broadway small insignificant changes to a normal eye in production had crept in. This is inevitable in a long run unless a director has an iron grip on the cast the whole time.

As Kazan wryly remembers: 'The cast called them improvements but I had to take these out to make it simpler and realer for the camera.'

Everyone was apprehensive as to how Marlon Brando (playing Stanley Kowalski) and Vivien Leigh would get on. He was at that time the unpredictable, mean, moody golden boy of Hollywood and she was the accepted royal lady of the British theatre. In those very early days both were a little wary of each other taking time out to sum each other up.

Kazan enjoyed the fact that they were two 'different kinds of animal' and parried differences with great sensitivity.

He says: 'It took her about three weeks to feel at home with Brando and then she really got to admire him although she knew that their techniques were as different as can be. They respected each other and certainly worked well together and still there was this difference that was valuable and which I used – that she came from another civilisation, from another way of life, and somehow that fitted into the way the characters were.'

Vivien Leigh had a different version of working with Kazan. She told David Lewin:

'Kazan saw Blanche differently from me; he was irritated by her. I could not share his view and I knew how it should be played after nine months on the stage. I did it my way and Kazan and I were finally in complete agreement.

'It took three months to make the film and I loved every second. I couldn't wait to get to the studio every morning and I hated to leave at night. The script stayed exactly as it had been written without changes and everyone knew it and wanted to help. Right down to the prop man who used to say to me: "What sort of things do you think Blanche would have on her table next to her bed?" There was such enthusiasm and efficiency and I don't always find it like that in British studios.'

In the beginning Vivien Leigh and Brando were unable to understand each other. As she said to David Lewin:

'I thought he was terribly affected. He used to say to me: "Why do you have to say good morning to everyone?" and I'd say, "Because it is a good morning and anyway it is a nice thing to say, so why not?"

'I got to understand him much better as he went on with the filming. He is such a good actor and when he wants to he can speak excellent English without a mumble. He is the only man I have ever met who can imitate Larry accurately. Larry is awfully difficult to imitate. Brando used to do speeches from *Henry V* and I closed my eyes and it could have been Larry.

'Brando also had a nice singing voice; he sang folk songs to us beautifully. I became great friends with all the American cast on *Streetcar* and I particularly liked Kim Hunter, who played my sister.'

Kazan is noted for 'nearly killing his actors with work'. By driving them with white hot intensity he produces from them a performance far deeper and more emotional than their natural ability would have given. And for this reason he is considered one of the greatest directors in the world today.

He and Vivien Leigh suddenly found this intensity together and enjoyed it.

'I admired her a great deal because she never stopped trying to be excellent,' he says today. 'She would never be satisfied and I think if I said to her, "let's do it again," she would have crawled through a field of broken glass to be as good as she could be. Everyone had to admire her.'

It was the same selfless efficiency as she had shown in fact in those very early Hollywood days in *Gone With the Wind*. Every director who has ever handled Vivien Leigh remembers her searching to improve on her performance.

As Kazan says: 'I didn't think that she was the most gifted person that I have ever worked with but she certainly was intelligent and honest. She was a person with experience in life and extremely candid and fair in her opinions. She felt that there would be the differences which were there and she felt she was right which is natural and correct that she should.'

'Her zest for living is I think peculiarly English and I think she made up with energy, desire and reach what she lacked perhaps in talent.

'After a while they all loved her. The damn crews are so used to beautiful women that they can turn against a beautiful woman in a day if they find her foolishly difficult. She was never anything of that. She was a wonderful professional and very soon everyone got the idea that this was a very fine person. She had her tastes and she liked some people better than others but that is how it should be. You shouldn't like everybody and why should you? And you shouldn't like everybody equally, that's absurd. Vivien had very definite opinions as to what was what.'

With her history of breakdowns the financiers were relieved to hear that Laurence Olivier would be in Hollywood at the same time. He was making *Sister Carrie* and so could take some of the nervous tension from Vivien after the day's shooting. There was someone to talk over minor upsets and to see that she took care of herself and got sufficient rest.

And for Vivien the return to Hollywood as Lady Olivier was not without significance. She still remembered her first visit when making *Gone With the Wind* when she lived in a house with high walls for the maximum privacy and on studio orders had to arrive and leave parties at a different time from Laurence Olivier.

Now all the Hollywood smart set was at her feet. And this she relished.

When she arrived her great friend Danny Kaye gave a

party that staggered even Hollywood by its opulence. Elia Kazan and Jack Warner were not amused. They ordered Vivien to go to bed early and stay away from parties. They did not want to take any chances for the film with which they hoped to win an Academy Award.

But the Oliviers did go to a children's party at Edna Best's. They intended to stay half an hour but so enjoyed themselves square dancing that they stayed several.

At weekends Vivien did not mix with the rest of the cast. It has never been her practice to do this and she made no exception this time. She and Olivier had taken a house across the road from Elia Kazan and every Sunday afternoon she held open house for the British colony in Hollywood.

Recalls Kazan: 'I was never a one to stay up late and I like to be in bed by eight on Sunday nights. But one of my most vivid memories of Vivien was with my daughter. She was about three years old at the time and she used to swim in Vivien and Larry's pool without anything on. I can see Vivien now swimming round the edge of the pool with my little daughter hanging on with her arms round her neck.'

'I had the time of my life with her,' Kazan says. 'It was more than just making a movie. It was a wonderful time and she enjoyed it too. After you got to know her she was a great pleasure to be with. After all we were both highly strung and temperamental people with strong tastes and with likes and dislikes. But somehow we got very close when we knew each other.'

All her acting career Vivien Leigh had fought to be recognised first as a stage actress and then as a film star.

'I'd rather be an Edith Evans any day than a Garbo,' she used to say.

But Elia Kazan has other views.

'I think that Vivien Leigh was a better film actress than a stage one. I have seen her on the stage a couple of times

143

and she always seemed to me to be rather small, but on the screen her gifts were very well tuned to the technique of making films,' he says.

Unlike the chaotic days in the filming of *Gone With the Wind* ten years before, Kazan was much more businesslike in his approach to filming and the sets unfolded themselves in more or less chronological order. This suited Vivien Leigh as it enabled her to develop Blanche's character in a natural way.

She and Kazan were so much in *rapport* by now that they were able to take a firm stand when Warner Brothers, in an effort to placate the Hay's Office, attempted to take liberties with the script.

Vivien had never been happy the way a compromise had been accepted in London. The Lord Chamberlain's office had been adamant in not allowing the word homosexual to be used. Though she had personally pleaded herself it had had to be handled like this.

Blanche would explain: 'I came into the room and there was my husband and . . .' Here she would break down sobbing. While there is every chance that an intimate theatre audience would know the play and therefore understand the implications, both Vivien Leigh and Elia Kazan felt that unless it was more fully understood millions of film goers round the world would miss the essence of the whole drama.

Tennessee Williams was called to Hollywood and production was held up while Warners, Williams, Kazan and to a minor degree Vivien Leigh argued it out.

In the end Tennessee Williams rewrote the speech and Blanche ended up by saying: 'He wasn't like other people.' It was a compromise that was completely unacceptable to Vivien Leigh but at least the film got under way again.

The success of the film is now cinema history and

ve the St James's Theatre' was one of
ien Leigh's many crusades. She is shown
ove) leading the march, (*right*) bawling out
member of the public who had the audacity
disagree with her, (*below*) talking with Mr
ix Fenston who bought the St James's
eatre and (*below, right*) taking a last look
the theatre which she and Sir Laurence
for eight years.

Paul Popper

Paul Popper

Paul Popper

From the career of Vivien Leigh, actress: (*above, left*) May 1945, a big success in *The Skin of ou Teeth*. (*Above, right*) January 1949 with Sir Laurence Olivier on the first night of *The School F Scandal*. (*Left*) 1945 with Flora Robson in the film version of Bernard Shaw' *Caesar and Cleopatra*.

admirers of Vivien Leigh felt that under the sensitive direction of Elia Kazan she had given one of the greatest performances of her career.

'She was determined to be wonderful and she was,' Elia Kazan says when looking back on making the film. 'She loved a good time. She loved to be among people. She was always very funny. Some people said she was bitchy. But bitchy to me is a very close synonym to candour. She always said her own mind. It was great fun to hear her because she would say things that people were thinking and didn't dare say. To talk to her was refreshing because you knew that other people felt the same way but she would just say it and then she would laugh. You would then realise that at the bottom she was not mean at all but the opposite. She was just interested in genuine relationships which mean truthful ones. I liked her.'

Vivien Leigh and Elia Kazan did not meet again for some time afterwards. She didn't go back to America and he didn't go to London.

'A long time had elapsed when I did see her. She had been sick and I was told that she had some mental trouble with breakdowns and one thing and another.

'I went to see her and I found her perfect. I found her very much in command of herself. She was just as entertaining and warm to be with. But then I kept hearing these stories that she had been mentally sick. But you are used to that in this kind of work when people have times in their lives when they are not as happy as they were. It is just normal.'

Vivien Leigh herself always regarded the filming of *Streetcar* as one of the forward points of her career.

Her greatest happiness was always when she had reached a new peak of her career. But it was in the ordinary everyday valleys that she found life difficult to cope with.

Cleopatra

WHETHER VIVIEN LEIGH was the most brilliant stage Cleopatra will be debated among theatre critics for years to come. But she was undoubtedly the sexiest.

'I would have loved to have been Cleopatra in real life – providing I could choose my own Antony,' she said discussing the Queen of the Nile to a journalist. And she meant it, for cloaked under that shimmering mantle of femininity was an astute and sometimes ruthless mind.

If it had not been for the Festival of Britain in 1951 it is doubtful whether London would ever have seen the Oliviers in their most daring theatrical adventure, the production of Shakespeare's *Antony and Cleopatra* and Shaw's *Caesar and Cleopatra* on alternate nights.

They had returned from Hollywood at the end of 1950 where Laurence Olivier had completed the film of *Carrie* and Vivien Leigh *A Streetcar Named Desire*. In just five months they had to find a major production to fill the St James's theatre for the opening of a glittering season when London was expected to be filled with overseas visitors.

It was designer Roger Furze who dreamed up the improbable idea of the two Cleopatras. His whim was first rejected and it was not until Vivien and her husband were in Paris for a few days that Olivier from his bed of 'flu grabbed the phone and called Furze in London. 'We are going ahead with that crazy idea of yours,' he said. Once Olivier had accepted the idea his infectious vitality did the rest and the 'flu vanished. Vivien was more cautious. She always enjoyed 'dressing up' – or undressing as in this case

– but could she find the right contrast between Shakespeare's calculating siren and Shaw's playful kitten? Costumes and make-up were superficial aids but there must be some more subtle way of differentiating between the two interpretations.

This she did through her voice. Laurence Olivier's vocal gymnastics had always been recognised and acclaimed by theatre critics but Vivien was as yet untried. She faced competition with actresses who had tried one or the other rôles but never the two together – Edith Evans, Peggy Ashcroft and even Mrs Patrick Campbell.

Together she and Olivier worked on switching her voices – one night she would play Shaw's Cleopatra in the upper register and the following night Shakespeare's in the lower. It was no mean feat for any actress. The alternating from comedy to tragedy on alternate nights was an added strain.

With all the intensity that she brought to her work, she began studying the character of Cleopatra. She read everything and she discussed Cleopatra with anyone she thought could advise her.

Talking to Maurice Zolotow later in America when the two productions were transported there Vivien Leigh explained:

'I don't think Shaw grasped Cleopatra as deeply as Shakespeare did. Shaw got the shrewdness, quickness, ambition of her character but he just wasn't taken by her passion, her emotion – and not only in love affairs. She was intense about everything. She had a fabulous collection of jewellery, gold, silver and even clothes. She was even intense about her dying. All her life she studied different poisons. She would have prisoners brought before her and she would try out various poisons on them. She found out that the quick poisons hurt too much and the tastier poisons took too long. Finally she found out that the bite of an asp was the least painful and it made you feel sleepy and you died without being in agony.'

Apart from the vocal differences Vivien studied and created her own make-up for the two rôles. For Shaw's sixteen-year-old Cleopatra she made her a petulant kitten by using rouge high on her cheekbones to make them plumper and kept her eyes wide, bright and feline. For the older Queen she applied a darker rouge down the jaw bones to give a harder, more sophisticated leanness and applied bright green kinetic eye make-up. She also studied every illustration she could find for costume detail but as always, like Mrs Patrick Campbell, historical details were adapted to suit herself. Once she stood six hours without a break during fittings.

As costume designer Audrey Cruddas explained: 'She insists that her costumes flatter her as a person rather than merely suit the character she is playing.'

It was one of the enigma's of Vivien Leigh's character that she thought of Shakespeare's Cleopatra as being the rôle for her and Shaw's as being too slight. She set her own aims so high that when people, whose opinion she would respect, would compliment her on the Shaw characterisation and not the Shakespeare she was despondent and unhappy. She thought that because *Antony and Cleopatra* was the better play her performance would naturally be better.

In describing Vivien in *Antony and Cleopatra*, *enfant terrible* of the theatre critics Kenneth Tynan, now a co-director of the National Theatre with Sir Laurence Olivier, wrote: 'She picks at the part with the daintiness of a débutante called upon to dismember a stag.

'Miss Leigh's limitations have wider repercussions than those of most actresses. Sir Laurence with that curious chivalry which sometimes blights the progress of every great actor gives me the impression that he subdues his blow-lamp ebullience to match her. Blunting his own iron precision, levelling away his towering authority he meets her half way. Antony climbs down and Cleopatra pats him on the head. A cat in fact can do more than look at a king; she can hypnotise him.'

W A Darlington was less concerned with connubial comparisons and wrote in the *Daily Telegraph* about *Antony and Cleopatra*:

'True she came a little short in the earlier scenes. She was never transported by passion to the pitch when she would have thrown away the world for its indulgence. But she has that special and rare type of beauty that lights into a glow on the stage and this carried her safely through. Later she succeeded by sheer good acting. Her dignity and power in the death scene were beyond anything we have hitherto seen from her.'

When the company went to America, transporting twenty-five tons of scenery, including the revolving stage built in England, the queen's barge, a light house and the fifteen-foot-long and seven-foot-high sphinx was a military operation. New York was agog with the sheer magnitude of the productions. When Cleopatra first entered in the moonlight between the paws of the sphinx and startled Caesar in paying his respects to the symbol of Egypt there was a ripple of emotion in every rhinestone-studded bosom of that chic first-night audience. And the following night when she committed suicide on the same spot where Antony had died they were convinced of the invincible greatness of the Oliviers. As the *New York Times* wrote:

'There has never been an Antony and Cleopatra to compare with this in New York in the last quarter of a century and there have not been many productions of any Shakespearean play that have approached this exalted quality.'

Pregnancy

AT THE AGE of forty-three when many women are grand-
mothers Vivien Leigh was astonished and apprehensive to
find that she was having a baby. This would be her second
child in twenty-two years and set the seal on a marriage
that *au fond* had everything – glamour, professional
success and riches.

The baby was expected in December 1956. The doctor
had assured Vivien that despite previous miscarriages there
was no reason why this child should not be strong and
healthy as she was going through a good period in her own
mental and physical health.

The first thing the Oliviers decided was that the flat
that they were renting from Sir William Walton, the
composer, was not suitable and they would need a place
big enough to accommodate baby and a nanny. They had
hoped to find a Georgian house in the precincts of Chelsea
with at least five bedrooms and a small garden. The nursery
was to be decorated in yellow and white – 'lovely sunny
colours,' Vivien Leigh said.

To the inquisitive Press who flocked to their flat in
Lowndes Place, Lady Olivier was more patient and amiable
than ever before. Neither she nor Sir Laurence had ever
had a very cosy relationship with the gossip-writing side of
the Press. They were both known at times to be distinctly
unco-operative. 'I will be continuing my part in *South Sea
Bubble* for several more weeks – no, I am not taking any
special precautions . . . yes, I do feel very excited and well
and naturally we are very happy.'

Unlike her usual reticence when talking to the Press about personal things she bubbled on:

'I don't mind whether it is a boy or girl but Sir Laurence would like a girl. Oh, you know men,' she laughed. 'They like to be comforted in their old age with a daughter.'

She went on to explain that Noël Coward, who wrote *South Sea Bubble*, was delighted.

'He wrote me to say that he felt in some strange way he was entirely responsible for the affair.

'I'm going to have to learn all over again being a mother – it has been so long since the last baby. And I'm no good at knitting.'

The Oliviers had never seemed so relaxed before and Vivien was no different from any other suburban mother-to-be.

She posed willingly for photographers, looking lovingly into Sir Laurence's eyes and he bent over as if to kiss her. Straightening himself up suddenly he said: 'Oh no – we are much too old to kiss.'

Benevolently Sir Laurence told reporters:

'Why I just adore babies.'

Even a name had been chosen – Kathryn if it was a girl although there was some discussion as to whether it would be Cathryn or Kathryn.

Everyone who knew the Oliviers was happy. Sir Laurence had never made a secret of the fact that he would have loved to have their own children. Each had had a child by their previous marriages – Vivien a daughter, Suzanne, and Laurence a son, Tarquin.

Looking incredibly slim in a blue linen suit Lady Olivier already had that bloom that pregnant women often acquire.

'This time I will get my maternity clothes made. If any designer can hide having a baby he is a genius,' she said good-naturedly.

When a pert reporter said:

'Will Marilyn Monroe be a godmother?' (she was arriving next day for the filming of *The Sleeping Prince*), Sir Laurence floundered:

'That's an interesting idea.'

'But, darling, they've already been chosen,' Vivien said quickly rescuing him.

For Laurence Olivier, apart from the baby excitement, it was a tremendously anxious time. For months he had been warned of the difficulties that lay ahead of him directing Marilyn Monroe.

When friends had asked Vivien Leigh why she was not following her usual policy and re-creating her stage success in *The Prince and the Show Girl*, she had replied with her usual candour:

'I'm too old, I'm afraid. Too old. It's all right on the stage. The audience is not too close and you can play younger parts. But you can't deceive the film cameras. They show up too much.'

In fact it was Vivien Leigh who suggested Marilyn Monroe to the author Terence Rattigan and Laurence Olivier after seeing her in the film *How to Marry a Millionaire*. Vivien was the first to realise that she was twelve years older than the effervescent Marilyn, then at the height of her career.

The Millers with twenty-seven suitcases were arriving at the airport on the Saturday morning and both the Oliviers were there to meet them. As the Press and photographers surged forward Vivien was jostled around in the frenzy.

The two stars met shyly.

'Are all your press conferences like this?' Vivien asked Marilyn.

'Well, this is a little quieter than some of them,' Marilyn giggled back.

From the airport everyone was swept along in an hilarious motor-cavalcade to the Parkside House in Englefield Green which the Millers had rented from Lord Moore.

It was all madly chummy. While Vivien looked on like a demure big sister, little sister Marilyn was flaunting her sex through her first tough English press conference.

'Yes, I am wearing a girdle to keep my stockings up' . . . 'I love the country, you know the birds and the bees' . . . 'I am going to buy a bicycle,' she prattled.

'Why, that's not necessary,' Sir Laurence broke in. 'I'll lend you mine, sweetie.'

'Oh, thanks, Larry – thanks a lot,' she gushed.

With her usual thoughtfulness Vivien Leigh had seen that the house looked 'lived in' and had filled it with flowers. The first night they all dined together.

Before a week's shooting was under way both Laurence Olivier and Vivien Leigh knew that whatever fun they had had in the stage production, the film version of *The Prince and the Showgirl* would be a nightmare. Psychic illness always overcame Marilyn when she felt under a strain.

Jack Cardiff, cameraman of the film, said:

'Sir Laurence was marvellous with Marilyn. He had been warned in New York never to shout at her. Never to show you are cross. She'll have a nervous breakdown and you won't get any work done at all. She'll be off for six weeks.'

As the weeks went by the climate got decidedly chillier on the set. In his biography[1] of Marilyn Monroe, Maurice Zolotow recalls the period:

'By now Monroe was openly and sarcastically addressing him (Laurence Olivier) as "Mister Sir". Gone was the "Larry" of yesteryear.'

On the set Laurence Olivier's manners were impeccable,

[1] *Marilyn Monroe* by Maurice Zolotow, W H Allen, 1961

but the strain was enormous and the only person he could really open up to was his wife, Vivien Leigh. At night, home exhausted from a frustrating day's shooting, he would unwind to her.

Vivien Leigh ended her *South Sea Bubble* run on the Saturday night, 13th August. Her doctors had agreed to the first week in August even though she was in fact four months pregnant, but Vivien decided to stay on a week longer.

The rôle of Lady Alexander, the governor's lady, was effortless. It was a gay Cowardish romp that required no great emotional strain. One minute she would be serving tea to the natives and the next she was whirling and twirling in a dance. After the show there was a farewell party for Vivien that also was in the nature of a welcome one for Elizabeth Sellars who was taking over the part.

On the Sunday Vivien had intended to go to Notley Abbey where she was going to spend much of her time while Laurence Olivier was filming.

In the evening she said that she was not feeling well. Two doctors were called. But it was too late. She had lost her baby.

On Monday Olivier dragged himself back to the studios and Monroe's tantrums and continued as if nothing had happened. It was not until the day's shooting was finished that the cast was told.

Marilyn, who had lost several babies herself and knew the disappointment, wired 'deepest sympathy' to Vivien.

Recalling, friends now say: 'She only wanted the baby for Larry's sake. Because of his absolute passion for children she would have given anything to have had his child.'

When film critic Donald Zec called on her soon afterwards he wrote:

'She lay in her big silk-draped bed like a fragile blossom. The room blazed with red, pink and yellow roses. She was wan, pale and infinitely sad. Two Siamese cats, Snow and Christmas, lay on the floor, also quiet.'

Every time a caller came the white coated housekeeper received the flowers and then with eyes filling with tears said: 'Sir Laurence and Lady Olivier are broken-hearted.'

A specially poignant note was that on the day that Vivien Leigh lost her child Hester Olivier (wife of Sir Laurence's brother, Dick, who lived in the cottage at Notley and managed the farm) had given birth to a six-pound baby girl. On hearing Vivien's news Hester had said from hospital:

'Maybe – maybe she would like to be the baby's god-mother.'

No one, not even the doctor, knew what exactly did go wrong. But it is a fact that Vivien had had a pretty hectic time that last month and had not spared herself.

She had arranged and been hostess at a supper party given by Terence Rattigan for the Arthur Millers and had not left till 2 am. Next day she gave both a matinée and evening performance.

She had also insisted on dressing up in top hat and white tie and tails, and appearing at a midnight charity performance with Laurence Olivier and John Mills.

It was a hotted up song and dance routine that would have tired anyone not in regular practice. With her passion for perfection Vivien had insisted on practising for thirty-five hours until her dancing was absolutely professional.

But all this was done with the doctor's knowledge. Medical experts say that once the tricky third month is over chances of a miscarriage after the fourth month are slight. And anyway she had felt so well.

In an interview with film writer David Lewin at the time, Sir Laurence said poignantly:

'We have tried to blame ourselves for this. We have tried to find a reason for what has happened. But Vivien lost her baby and I do not think it is because she went on working too long. It is just bad, bad luck. Fate.

'It is natural to try and find reasons. When the baby was first starting we went to see our doctors and asked what we should do. The doctors' advice was, carry on till the first week in August. Now it is the second week. Is it too long?'

Two weeks later, looking pale and tired, Vivien Leigh could not even then escape the photographers. For three minutes she smiled as she stood on the steps of the Lowndes Place house. Then suddenly, without any warning, she rushed inside.

A woman friend came to the door.

'Miss Leigh is terribly upset and she thanks you for coming.'

A fortnight later in a well-kept secret that even the Press did not find out she left for Italy to stay at Rex Harrison's house at Portofino. Lili Palmer, his wife then, had moved to friends so that Vivien could have the place to herself.

She read, pottered in the garden and rested. Every day Sir Laurence phoned.

It was a period for quiet reflection. One thing is fairly certain. Had Vivien Leigh had her baby it is extremely doubtful that the Oliviers' marriage would ever have ended just four years later.

A Personal Crusade

THE ST JAMES's Theatre was to be pulled down to make way for a modern office block. There had been rumours but now it was fact. In desperation Vivien Leigh began to marshal her own private army to make a protest against the decision. She felt strongly that if public opinion could be roused the 114-year-old St James's could be saved. She decided on a protest march to Whitehall.

It was a forlorn little procession in July 1957 that wended its way from Fleet Street down the Strand en route to Westminster. There was Vivien Leigh, immaculate in a grey and blue Balmain dress with perky butcher blue beret on the back of her head, the sixty-eight-year-old actress Athene Seyler and the Oliviers' great personal friend theatre critic Alan ('Jock') Dent, his leonine grey head towering over his two dollies. Laurence Olivier was not in the procession.

Before setting off they bravely posed on the edge of the Fleet Street pavement for some Canadian newspaper photographers. Vivien was gleeful as she clanged a bell borrowed from a pub near the Stoll Theatre where the Oliviers were appearing in *Titus Andronicus*. She also carried a small home-made poster signed by Dame Edith Evans and character actor Felix Aylmer.

What was wrong is that the trio appeared to be under-rehearsed. Instead of a great theatrical crusade it had turned into a Ralph Lynn farce.

After the first sprightly few yards the trio developed into an amble and swapped theatre gossip. Every now and then Vivien would remember the cause and give her bell an extra flourish. To a cruising Bentley alongside she shouted encouragement, 'Come on, Bernard!'

He turned out to be the Oliviers' liveried chauffeur who was waiting to take Vivien Leigh on to a lunch date.

If she had hoped to impress the lethargic London public, it was a real flop. The legal gentlemen in their gowns, en route from the Temple to the Law Courts, scarcely raised their heads. The general public treated the trio as harmless nut cases.

Vivien Leigh herself was astonished at the apathy.

'I was amazed at the lack of interest in our little demonstration. I have decided that if I want a quiet holiday and a rest the thing to do is to walk up the Strand carrying a sandwich board.'

Three days later she was to make one of her most dramatic and unrehearsed appearances ever. She had been invited by the Earl of Bessborough to hear the debate in the House of Lords calling for more state aid for the arts. Again she dressed with her usual exquisite care – a vivid green (her lucky colour) and black dress and small white halo hat.

Sitting in Black Rod's box below the bar in that august panelled chamber she was told that Nikita Kruschev and Marshal Bulganin had occupied the very same red leather chairs the year before. Surrounded by the noble lords Vivien Leigh looked like a very small, determined doll.

Lord Blackford, ninth in line of Speakers, had scarcely finished his speech when suddenly the little lady rose to her feet and in a loud back-row-of-the-stalls voice called out: 'My Lords I wish to protest against the St James's Theatre being demolished.'

Startled peers turned round to look at the intruder. Sadly few, if any, recognised her. Lieutenant-General Sir

Brian Horrocks sprang to his feet, took her firmly by the arm and persuaded her to silence.

'Now I will have to ask you to leave,' he whispered.

'Certainly,' replied Lady Olivier perkily. 'I have to go to the theatre.'

Forty-five minutes later at the Stoll Theatre, dressed in her Grecian robe for her rôle of Lavinia in *Titus Andronicus*, she explained:

'I went to the House as the personal guest of Lord Bessborough. I know quite a number of the members socially and at tea-time I had a little party with seven of them. My Lords were most charming over the tea cups. Then I went back to listen to Lord Bessborough's speech. My husband (Olivier takes longer to make-up than his wife) had left me at 6.30 and I got angrier and angrier as I listened. Suddenly I found myself on my feet. I felt terribly nervous. I have never played to an audience who seemed so unmoved. It was very embarrassing.

'I still felt extremely nervous as I walked out. There was such an absolute silence. It was a matter of impulse. I feel very passionately about the St James's Theatre but I went along with the intention of listening to the debate. It was as I listened that I got angrier and angrier.'

She continued and became even more excitable:

'If the St James's were pulled down I will leave England and act in other countries. England is no place for actors and actresses. I have paid enough money in taxes during my years on the stage. I can act in German, French, Italian – and maybe even Serbian.'

At this moment a slightly embarrassed Laurence Olivier, who had been eavesdropping on this tirade, stuck his head out of his dressing room and added, not without tolerance, 'Well, I wouldn't exactly say that.'

Whatever Laurence Olivier thought about his wife's

impulsiveness no one knew. Nor what he said in private to her. His only public comment was: 'I think it was a very sweet and gallant thing to do. What did I say when she told me? Nothing. I just gave her a kiss.'

Last word came from the far from contrite Vivien: 'It was the least effective performance that I have ever given.' Next day she received telegrams from dozens of people who all applauded her outburst.

Though she vehemently denied that she had planned to protest in the House of Lords the *Manchester Guardian* had in fact been tipped off on the night before that Vivien Leigh was going to speak.

A few days later Vivien Leigh scored her first real St James's triumph. She had written to Sir Winston Churchill asking for his support. As it happened Lady Churchill had booked seats for *Titus Andronicus* for the day that Sir Sir Winston had received her letter. It was a *cri de cœur*, and Vivien also reminded him how he had seen their two productions of Shakespeare's *Antony and Cleopatra* and Shaw's *Caesar and Cleopatra* when they were staged at the St James's.

Afterwards backstage she had fully intended to lobby Sir Winston but as she said: 'Everything depended on whether I got the opportunity to put my case. And I didn't.' Sensing a spirited performance, Granada television a few days later offered Vivien Leigh time in their People and Places programme.

It was a disaster. Just when she became eloquent, suddenly the voice of Elaine Grand from the Manchester Studio butted in: 'Thank you very much, Miss Leigh.'

Vivien Leigh was not used to being interrupted. She left the studio in anger. 'I won't go in front of that nasty machine for a long time to come. I understood that I had three minutes to state my case. I don't know how much I

One of her first stage rôles was in the 1937 London production of *Hamlet*. She is shown (*left*) in a scene from that production with actor George Howell. A year later (*bottom, left*) she was clowning as a busker with Charles Laughton in the film *Holborn Empire*. In 1940 she and Laurence Olivier took *Romeo and Juliet* on tour in America, probably the least successful tour they ever made together. This picture (*bottom, right*) is from the Chicago production of the play.

Two of the most famous scenes from *Gone With the Wind*.

did get but it didn't seem as much as that. In fact it was just two and a half minutes.'

Once more a St James's protest had failed.

By now the identity of the backer of the Mayflower Project, the company behind the purchase of the St James's Theatre, who intended to pull it down and erect a seven-storey block of offices, had leaked out.

It was Felix Fenston, one of the most influential property millionaires in London. He was obviously the man to approach.

In one of her rare moods of perversity, Vivien Leigh announced through the Press:

'I'll see him. But he must ask me. He's the gentleman – he should make the approaches. I'll give him until Saturday afternoon to do his stuff. If he doesn't then, by heavens, I'll go for him.'

If the words have a Shakespearean ring about them the lady is to be excused. She was angry, very angry.

Earlier she had illogically appealed to the Trade Unionists to refuse to pull down the St James's. 'While there are houses waiting to be built for the homeless why attack a theatre,' she implored.

Laurence Olivier remained quiet throughout these lively announcements. While approving in principle of his wife's objection, friends say that he felt that there must be another way to handle the matter instead of Vivien's barnstorming.

Even Giles, the celebrated *Sunday Express* cartoonist, joined in the fun.

He drew a cartoon of Vivien Leigh in her sitting room answering the telephone:

'Vivien dear, repeat after Larry, I will be a good girl and come straight to rehearsals. I must not join protest marches on the way. I must not call out in the House of Lords and wake everyone up. . . .'

When Felix Fenston read of Vivien's request to meet him he readily agreed.

On 18th July they met in the sombre five-storey house in Belgravia where Mr Fenston lived. Vivien Leigh wore the same outfit in which she had made her protest at the House of Lords and bearded Mr Fenston chose a dark green and black flecked suit.

'I don't remember too closely now what we did say,' Fenston says. 'But at least we appeared to be on the same side in that it was a shame that this historic theatre would have to come down, but I didn't think it was financially possible to save it.

'The theatre had been up for sale for some considerable time and presumably it was open to others besides myself to make arrangements to purchase it if they wanted. But by now it was too late.

'As a theatre it was not practical. It had a lot of awkward pillars and, if your seat was behind them, you simply couldn't see. I understood that Gilbert Miller and Prince Littler had had losses over the twenty-seven years' lease.'

The meeting was short but as they left, to the photographers' delight, Vivien announced maternally: 'Come along, Felix dear. Shall I drop you or will you drop me?'

In forty-seven minutes they had bridged the Christian name barrier if nothing else.

A second conference was held with real cloak-and-dagger secrecy. Rendezvous X was chosen in Cadogan Place, the house of Miss Fiore de Henriques, who was sculpting a head of Vivien at the time.

Why? It is difficult to understand because Fleet Street seemed to have everything well taped even to the time of the principal players' arrivals. The small street with its pastel painted houses was jammed with reporters and photographers.

At 2.20 pm in a grey lounge suit, looking more like a successful insurance salesman, Laurence Olivier arrived on foot with head bent in thought.

At 2.30 the front door was opened and cameras raised. It was a false alarm. The green-frocked maid called Jennifer slipped out and popped round the corner for a bottle of brandy and cigarettes.

Although she lived but five minutes walking distance away, at 2.40 pm Vivien Leigh swept into view in her black and chocolate Bentley with its name plate VLO 1.

At 2.46 pm Fenston telephoned to apologise that he would be a little late. He made it by 3 pm driving his own little black car. Taking one look at the bunch of Press, he nipped smartly round the corner and through the kitchen door. At 3.5 p m, behind drawn blinds, the conference began.

At 3.35 a plump woman in a pink blouse and white coat stepped up smartly and rang the bell. There was no reply. Bewildered she turned to a reporter and asked:

'Is Miss Leigh having her head done?'

The comments are unprintable.

At 3.47 Miss de Henriques in white artist's smock and black and white check trousers opened the door and announced grandly:

'They're coming out.'

Down the steps they went giving a spirited performance – the laughing Vivien and the benign millionaire. Keeping up the bright chatter Vivien popped into Fenston's car and off they drove to the St James's. She wanted him to see the theatre and feel the atmosphere.

Here it was all very sentimental. Another batch of Press, fresh to the story, were waiting. They were delighted when Lady Olivier posed with Felix Fenston kissing her!

She then rushed into the theatre, asked stagehand Fred Hicks for lights and curtains up and, looking into the silent auditorium, announced solemnly:'How nice it is.'

It was obvious that Vivien Leigh was moved. Nostalgically, like a small girl, she peered up at the boxes and said: 'We papered the walls and the boxes. I know some seats are not very good for seeing but it would cost far less to put them right than build something new.'

Mr Fenston said nothing Later in the evening he told the Press:

'If my associate company had not made an offer to develop the site it would undoubtedly have been bought by one of the other property developers. The figures involved now make it impossible to my mind for the theatre to continue and be run other than at a substantial loss.

'I am told that the London County Council are concerned that the theatre does not comply with present-day by-laws. They would have considerable difficulty in granting a licence.'

Looking back with everything now in its right perspective it was a brave show on Vivien Leigh's part but someone should have warned her that most millionaires have hearts of shining steel.

Mr Fenston had been in negotiation with the National Coal Board over the St James's site long before the Oliviers had begun their Save the Theatre campaign – a point he had apparently omitted to tell Vivien Leigh at their various meetings.

As Felix Fenston said: 'I met Lady Olivier because she wanted it. Just a matter of courtesy.'

At the Coal Board itself where everyone had remained silent during the last days of passion a spokesman said: 'Must say we're glad the news didn't break earlier. Shouldn't have liked to get involved with Lady Olivier.'

Later, Mr Fenston asked the Oliviers to dinner:

'I think we discussed the theatre and arts in general. I don't really remember,' he says now.

Vivien Leigh's appearance at the House of Lords had not been in vain. The House by twenty-two votes to eighteen carried a resolution against Government advice urging a standstill at the St James's.

Lord Silkin and Lord Pakenham proved Miss Leigh's staunchest supporters. Lord Silkin announced in the House that Mr Huntington Hartford, of the Great Atlantic and Pacific Tea Company and one of America's richest philanthropists, had promised substantial aid.

When she heard about the House of Lords' vote Vivien Leigh clapped her hands like a little girl and said: 'I daren't go in there again. But it is simply thrilling.'

When told, just before going on the stage at the Stoll, of the cables that had been received from Huntington, Vivien said:

'I am so excited about it all. Let's drink a toast to Mr Hartford and Mr Cort (another American millionaire whom she thought had also promised aid). I haven't met Mr Cort but I have met Mr Hartford once at a party in New York.

'Why are there no English millionaires who want to save the St James's? I know Mr Hartford's wife [actress Marjorie Steele] through a very great friend, Constance Collier. They are filled with charm and dough.'

Marjorie Steele had played in *Sabina Fair* at the St James's three years previously and for this reason Vivien thought they might be sentimental about the theatre.

In New York, 'Hunt' Hartford had announced that he was prepared to put up the sum of £34,000 towards saving the theatre. Mr Cort later denied anything about his cable. There had been a complete misunderstanding he said.

This left the Oliviers to find the additional £350,000 to save the theatre. The company Viarex Property Investment Co, of which Mr Fenston is a shareholder, also had to be satisfied that in addition to this minimum sum that there would be an organisation able to undertake the management of the theatre in perpetuity.

At no time was there ever any question of Felix Fenston supplying financial aid to saving the St James's. 'There are more charity letters in the post than business ones these days,' he said. 'My business is real estate and not the theatre.

'Presumably there are people with money who would have liked to have saved the theatre and, in the early days before the lease ran out and serious negotiations begun, it could have been arranged. But it was all far too late when I came in.'

Undoubtedly the Oliviers themselves were prepared to invest some money in the St James's, and possibly there were other members of the acting profession who would have, but £350,000 was a formidable sum for any troupe of players to find.

Rumours

IT WAS JULY 1957 and the time seemed right again to Vivien Leigh for yet another march on Whitehall to save St James's Theatre. This time it would be rehearsed and organised with military precision.

Whenever it had anything to do with her professional life, or causes dear to her heart, Vivien Leigh had a genius for publicity. Although she hated her private life being exposed and gave fewer interviews than any other star of her magnitude (except perhaps Garbo), she proved extremely efficient with the St James's. The Press always knew well in advance what her next move would be.

The day before the great assault on Whitehall she gave a press conference and said:

'There were only three of us last time. But this time we are frightfully well organised. We are starting at eleven o'clock and marching to St Martin's in the Fields. The vicar there has lent us his courtyard. But he added would we please not be too loud because there is a wedding in the church at the same time. It wouldn't do if angry actors were shouting, "I won't", just when the bride is saying, "I will".'

They had hoped to make the meeting in Trafalgar Square but mass meetings are not permitted there until after 2 pm, by which time many actors are at their matinées.

It was wet and cold but Vivien in pale raincoat and rainhat was triumphant as she walked among the three hundred actors and fans who had gathered outside the St James's Theatre.

'A wonderful turn out. Most encouraging,' she commented with the precision of a general.

Soon everyone was ready. There was a band in front and two young men led the procession carrying a banner which read: 'Save the St James's Theatre. Public meeting 11.45 today at St Martin's Churchyard.'

While everybody was getting marshalled into place a man went up to Vivien Leigh and said:

'I admire you Lady Olivier but I don't agree.'

Her angelic face turned white with rage as she snapped back:

'Pipe down then. You're a silly fool.'

Laurence Olivier remarked to a nearby friend:

'I'm thinking of changing my name to Mr Pankhurst.'

The Oliviers led the procession, Vivien waving to everyone like a happy schoolgirl on a day's outing.

To boost her morale she carried a letter she had received from Sir Winston Churchill in her pocket.

'If – as seems possible – a fund is needed I shall be glad to subscribe £500,' he wrote. 'I hope you will succeed although as a Parliamentarian I cannot approve of your disorderly methods.'

On they marched to the booming of the band with Vivien looking back every now and then to see that everyone was in order.

Before setting out she had told the ranks:

'We have been asked by the police to make no further disturbance than necessary as it interrupts the traffic.'

At St Martin's in the Fields it all fizzled out but this time at least Londoners had not ignored them.

When asked by a frivolous reporter if she intended to chain herself to any railings she replied, with a great burst of laughter: 'I hate chains – except gold ones. Let's all go and have a drink at the pub.'

Summing up the protest Vivien Leigh said:

'Excellent. We will not give up our fight and today's turn-out in the rain was most encouraging. But,' she added, 'my feet are killing me.'

The next step was a small deputation consisting of Vivian Leigh, Laurence Olivier and actor Felix Aylmer, then president of Equity, who called on Mr Henry Brooke, Minister of Housing.

Vivien Leigh had taken great care with her dress and looked supremely feminine in pale coral pink with a black hat. A black eye patch, to cover an infected eye, added drama to her pale, poised face.

The interview was brief and perhaps pointless. Commenting afterwards Felix Aylmer said:

'Although Mr Brooke assured our deputation that the Government had a great concern for the theatre generally, he seemed to feel that the St James's had slipped through the net.'

In the early hours of 27th July the St James's Theatre had its farewell party.

It was a very sad occasion for all those present and for London theatregoers in general. Sir George Alexander had made this intimate little theatre famous in the nineties, and it was here that he had presented Oscar Wilde's greatest successes. It had also once been in the hands of the Kendalls and even Barnum, the circus king, had once managed it.

Everyone was near to tears that last night.

With her attention to detail Vivien Leigh had arrived early with bottles of vintage champagne. If the St James's had to go then the old theatre would close with dignity.

Perhaps one of those present who felt it most was Laurence Olivier. He was very quiet 'and looked infinitely sad', one of the onlookers said.

The curtains were pulled and all those there looked out

into the auditorium for the last time. Someone uncorked the champagne and a spurt hit Vivien Leigh in the eye.

She dried her eyes and dabbed it behind her ears for good luck. The tension was broken.

Soon afterwards the demolition squads moved in on the proud old theatre. The little red plush seats and the gold were all smothered with dust and rubble.

The spirit of St James's Theatre had departed. The only memory that remains to the two people who tried to save its life – Vivien Leigh and Laurence Olivier – is a plaque of their profiles along with Prince Littler and Gilbert Murray which are inset in the entrance hall of the great glass block that rose out of the ashes.

It is characteristic of Vivien Leigh's honesty that she bore Felix Fenston no malice afterwards and in fact would hear no criticism of him.

'A lot of people are trying to make out Mr Fenston as the villain of this piece. I don't think he is at all. He is a very charming man and he is interested in the arts. I don't think our cause is lost by any means,' she said.

As though she had not churned up enough publicity, on 8th August 1957 unwittingly Vivien Leigh became the centre of one of the strangest attacks any woman member of Parliament has made on another woman.

Quite naturally she told friends that she was going with her first husband, Leigh Holman, and their daughter on a holiday to Italy. Laurence Olivier who loved a quiet holiday was taking his son Tarquin (by his first marriage to Jill Esmond) to Scotland. From close friends the news sifted to acquaintances and finally the Press heard of it.

To the five sophisticated people concerned it seemed a perfectly natural thing to do. They all loved and respected each other very much. Until her death Vivien Leigh regarded her first husband as one of her closest confidants and dearest friends and all through the years they had been in constant touch with each other.

Vivien loved travelling and lazing in the sun, Suzanne adored being with her parents and Sir Laurence and Tarquin enjoyed the rigours of a small hotel at Kyle on Lochalsh.

But they had not reckoned on the tenacious Mrs Mann, Labour Member of Parliament for Coatbridge and Airdrie.

At the National Conference on Social Work in Edinburgh she had galvanised a sleepy audience by suddenly announcing:

'There is a woman who took the House of Lords by storm and she has gone off on holiday with her first husband. Her second husband is on holiday elsewhere.

'I understand the lady got tea after she created the sensation in the House of Lords' (actually she got the tea beforehand). 'If she will accept an invitation from me I will give her tea in the House of Commons and tell her what I think of her.

'It is a terrible example for people who occupy high places in life to place before our young children today.'

Her speech had all the ring of melodrama about it of *The Painted Lady* or *The Scarlet Letter*.

Little did Mrs Mann know that in fact Lady Olivier and Mr Holman were in the habit of spending many weekends together. Either he would go to Notley Abbey or she would stay at his cottage in a Buckinghamshire village, an arrangement that everyone found most agreeable.

At the time Lady Olivier and her ex-husband were totally unaware of the rumpus they had caused as they travelled through Italy. In London storm clouds gathered. The benign BBC interviewer Cliff Michelmore invited Mrs Mann on his television programme to explain her attitude.

'This seems to me to be an example of friendly behaviour between two people. Why are you so upset about it?' he asked.

Mrs Mann replied in that matter-of-fact voice of hers:

'It indicates to me that divorce has been too easy. If a woman can find her ex-husband so congenial on holiday she should not have thrown in the towel so quickly when they married.'

By this time cosmopolitan Londoners were chuckling over their breakfast papers, and friends were just longing to know how Vivien would handle this one.

It was at a hotel on Lake Garda, where she shared a room with her daughter, that Lady Olivier finally heard the news through a telephone call from a London newspaper. She listened and commented grimly:

'At least she didn't mention my name.'

In the middle of dinner she promptly sent off a cable in well-chosen words to friends in England for distribution to the Press. It said:

'Criticism ill-considered and unmannerly. Presence our daughter gives explanation holiday to any reasonable person.'

Mr Holman seemed to regard the whole affair with mild amusement and refused to be brought in for comment except to say:

'It is possible we will do this regularly. We enjoyed it this year except perhaps for the bad joke.'

Explained Lady Olivier with her usual candour:

'We've spent holidays together before. Why this sudden rush of publicity. A divorce doesn't mean that people must dislike each other. We certainly don't – we're the best of friends – and we're having this holiday as we have had others for the sake of our daughter.'

When the *Daily Herald*, Labour's own voice, in a blockbusting leader demanded that Mrs Mann apologise because of her unjustified criticism she retired to her Clydeside fortress and said:

'I have no intention of apologising. Vivien Leigh has not asked for an apology and she wouldn't get one if she did! I am not interested in Miss Leigh as a person and there was no personal attack. There are just too many divorces, too many people chucking in marriage too easily. Ordinary wives may well say: "If they chuck it up with their husbands why should I stick on with this poultice of mine".'

Mrs Mann seemed totally unaware that in fact Vivien Leigh had chucked this particular poultice in 1937, and many soothing years had gone by.

Laurence Olivier had intended to join his wife and step-daughter in Yugoslavia but on his return from Scotland he found Laurence Olivier Productions stacked with work that needed his immediate attention. He also went immediately into rehearsal for John Osborne's *The Entertainer*, and at the same time was preparing the script for his film of *Macbeth*.

President Tito had asked the Oliviers to be his guest. They were to have met Tito and Mme Tito at Dubrovnik, the beautiful Dalmatian resort where they were to have stayed at the government guest house 'Villa Scheherazade'.

But without Laurence Olivier, Vivien Leigh felt unsure of how to handle any complications that may arise. Instead she slipped into Western Yugoslavia from Venice and stayed only three days. She then escaped to stay at Rex Harrison's villa at Portofino.

It was always a standing invitation from Rex Harrison that the Oliviers could use his villa any time they liked as Vivien Leigh and his late wife, Kay Kendall, had been the closest of friends.

On the way back mother and daughter stopped off at all

173

their special restaurants through France, including La Bonne Auberge in Antibes. She ordered one of her favourite dishes, partridges cooked in red cabbage. At the Hotel de la Côte d'Or in Saulieu near Dijon she had their special sea food dish in shrimp sauce which was always a great favourite with Laurence Olivier. Chef Dulman who had known him for many years gave her half a dozen bottles of vintage wine to take back as a gift.

In gay mood the chef and Lady Olivier sat down and wrote a wish-you-were-here postcard to Sir Laurence.

Looking sun tanned, healthy and in a marvellous mood the travellers arrived back on 29th August – to yet another storm.

Wearing a blue linen suit and flat-heeled shoes Lady Olivier came down the car ramp of the plane from Le Touquet ahead of her cream convertible with its number plate VLO 123 to be greeted once again by reporters.

'What do you have to say to the rumours that you and Sir Laurence are to have a "trial separation"?' one bold reporter asked.

When angry, Vivien Leigh's eyes become steely and exquisitely hard like emeralds.

'What rumours are these? I did not hear them in France or Italy,' she said. 'Anyway people have been saying for the last seventeen years that Larry and I would part.'

Her daughter Suzanne broke in at this stage.

'Tell them that the rumours are all nonsense.'

In fact Lady Olivier had heard the rumours in Paris and was therefore prepared.

In Paris she had told a reporter of the *Daily Express*:

'I am not contemplating divorce or separation any more now than at any time before. I am quite happy with things as they are.'

On the tarmac the persistent reporter probed:

'Are you expecting Sir Laurence to meet you?'

Again the diplomatic snap-back:

'Of course not. He has to rehearse in the evenings. I have bought him home some wine, shirts, shoes and collars. I love him. . . .'

At that strategic moment a car swept on to the apron and out jumped Olivier. The plane had in fact landed twenty minutes ahead of schedule.

In front of the astonished reporters they hugged and kissed with Suzanne looking on proudly.

Sir Laurence's comment on the rumours was succinct:

'I have no comment to make on a thing which does not exist.'

They then went off arm in arm to her car.

That silenced the rumours – this time.

Breakdown

JUST BEFORE SHE died in 1967, Vivien Leigh said wistfully to a friend: 'I have made my last film. Life is too short to work so hard. I want to go back to Ceylon again – I want to see it again. After all it does hold a lot of memories for me, some happy and some not so happy.'

When the script of *Elephant Walk* was completed, producer Irving Asher and director William Dieterie had only one acting couple in mind – the Oliviers. With this team they felt assured of a box-office success and, according to studio gossip, were willing to pay £140,000 for Olivier's services and £58,000 for Vivien Leigh.

At the time Vivien was available but as Olivier was still embroiled in his film *The Beggars' Opera*, and needed a rest, a substitute for the part of the egotistic, bicycle-polo tea planter had to be found. Olivier suggested Peter Finch. Looking back on the film a few years later Finch was to say: 'I was depressed the whole time I was in Hollywood making *Elephant Walk*. Everybody seemed so scared of losing their job or losing face or something.'

Before the final signature to the contract, Irving Asher flew to England to seek Olivier's advice on whether, with her history of ill-health, Vivien could stand the strain of filming in the heat of Ceylon for a month before going to Hollywood.

'I believe it will do her a world of good. A new environment and an interesting rôle. She has completely recovered from the tuberculosis,' Olivier replied.

When she first read the script, Vivien Leigh said: 'Oh

the bliss of not having to go mad, commit suicide or contemplate murder.'

It was a last-stronghold-of-the-Empire, hackneyed plot of a rich highbrow tea planter taking a middle-brow bride back to Ceylon – to a house of Oriental palace dimensions with all mod cons. When the wife finds that her husband not only suffers from father fixations, but is addicted to playing bicycle-polo along the marble corridors, she temporarily falls for the husband's first assistant, played in the film by Dana Andrews. Through cholera, monsoon and a stampede of elephants, true love wins through.

The heat and humidity in Ceylon in February 1953 were overpowering. The cycle of one of Vivien Leigh's manic depressive phases had already begun when she arrived. She could not sleep, she was restless and she burned herself up day and night.

All this took its toll on her strength and naturally her looks – the sheer weariness of working all day and staying up all night.

In one scene in the film she had to appear with a live cobra round her neck. With her intensity for getting the shot right she wore out two cobras that day – one in the morning and one in the afternoon.

When producer Irving Asher tactfully told her that she must ease off and take more rest, if for no other reason than the searing technicolor cameras spared no lines on the face, she shrugged him off: 'I am no longer young. I shouldn't look like a girl.'

With the outside shots completed (many of the long shots of Vivien still remain in the film), the unit was due back in Hollywood to finish the picture.

Despite the heat Vivien was emotionally upset at leaving this beautiful island, and facing the realities of push-button studio efficiency in Los Angeles.

The seventy-two-hour flight from Ceylon to Hollywood was especially gruelling for her. Exhausted and with tensions mounting she arrived in Hollywood in a near state of collapse. Ever since 1942 when one of the engines of the aircraft the Oliviers were flying in caught fire, and the plane had to make an emergency landing near Boston, she had feared long over-water flights.

The cycle of people suffering from manic depression begins with the manic period. During this time their pace of living greatly accelerates. They cannot sleep, alcohol affects them easily and they become touchy and argumentative. When the illness reaches its peak, they often become angry, break up furniture and resort to violence. After the climax comes weeks of depression when their energy is low, they have no appetite, cry a lot, appear withdrawn and have no wish to speak, or even to live. Vivien Leigh once described it as feeling 'like an amoeba at the bottom of the sea'.

Vivien Leigh's crisis mounted all during the first week of filming and finally hit her in the second week. Los Angeles gossip has it that confused, ill and distraught, she locked herself in her house and refused to open the door.

The studio called in David Niven, knowing that if anyone could influence and calm Vivien he could as their friendship stretched back to pre-war days. Niven and the Oliviers had always been immensely good friends.

Today Niven says: 'It's true, I am the only one who really knows what happened and I prefer to draw a veil over that period.'

David Niven and the studio brought in a doctor and nurse, and decided that Laurence Olivier, who was holidaying in Ischia, would have to be notified and consulted.

Dr Francis Macdonald, Vivien's doctor at the time, explained: 'Vivien Leigh's frequent nervous breakdowns must on no account be confused with insanity. They are just temporary mental aberrations and the brain in order to recover needs the same kind of care as any other part of the body – such as an arm or leg – if it becomes affected. The most important thing is complete rest and sleep.

'One of her tendencies has been an elaborate consideration for the wishes of other people I hear. After dinner one night after a day's filming, for instance, she insisted on doing all the dishes herself because she said the maid looked tired.'

Louella Parsons, referring to the illness, said: 'One of the curious phases was her compulsion to do housework and the feeling that she must sweep, dust and empty the ashtrays herself although she had plenty of servants.'

On the set in between fits of weeping she walked around reciting the Blanche dialogues from *Streetcar Named Desire* over and over again. She became such that she could not recognise the people around her at the studio and called Peter Finch 'Larry'. Distraught and bewildered the cast watched her near collapsing point, weeping and sighing: 'I want to be a grandmother. I want my daughter Suzanne to marry so that I can be a grandmother.'

It seemed that no one could help her. She was far beyond the orbit of normal human relationships. Only medical skill could help now. Paramount issued a terse announcement, stating that the production had closed down for a few days to give Miss Leigh a chance to recover.

At the Los Angeles airport, David Niven met Laurence Olivier, who in that pre-jet era had taken something like three days to get there from Ischia. After seeing his wife, Olivier and three doctors agreed that she would have to leave the film and, with her temperament, the sooner she got back to England the better.

After only two and a half weeks in Hollywood, she was

taken to the airport under sedation and flew with two nurses to New York. Their old friend Danny Kaye had been alerted by Olivier and met them at the plane. The BOAC plane for London had only five minutes to go, after specially waiting twenty minutes at La Guardia airport when Danny Kaye's car drove up. He and Olivier sat in the back seat and across their knees, on a blanket, lay the distraught Vivien, her head cradled in her husband's arms.

A stretcher stood waiting and a steward tried to lift Vivien from the car to the bed. Angrily, she pushed him away, tore loose from her escorts and collapsed on the floor of the car weeping.

Everyone pleaded with her but she just shook her head from side to side in desperation. Time and again, Olivier with gentle patience, leaned in to coax her, but like a frightened animal she warded him off.

Finally she straightened, pulled out her compact and put on her lipstick. But she still would not move. She had mistaken the crowds of normal airport plane spotters as being there to see her and pathetically cringed back into the car. Finally completely spent, she was almost dragged out of the car.

And then came the perilous walk to the airliner steps which she was determined to make. In her dark brown mink coat, her eyes puffy from weeping, and clinging to Olivier's arm, she slowly reached the steps. Only once did she turn that elfin profile to photographers but Olivier quickly hurried her on. It was more a reflex action on her part than one pertaining to the present situation.

Finally when she made the top step, clutching her bouquet of red roses, she turned and waved to the crowd, saying: 'I'm sorry, folks.' Again, even in such a crisis those perfect manners were evident.

In a curtained-off part of the plane, under sedation, she began the journey back to England with Olivier caring for and comforting her. On arrival she was met by an ambulance and taken to the Netherne Hospital for nervous disorders at Coulsdon in Surrey. She was allowed no flowers, no radio, no visitors, and shock treatment was administered. Through the half-drawn cretonne curtains, she lay half-conscious, looking out on to fields and a pine copse. The recovery had begun.

In a state of utter physical and mental depression, verging on a nervous breakdown, Olivier flew back to Italy to resume his holiday. There was nothing more he could do at the time.

Vivien Leigh had received £30,000 of her salary from the film when she left it and she later offered to pay this back. The twenty-one-year-old Elizabeth Taylor had taken over her rôle and in a film, which finally cost £1,200,000, Vivien's salary was negligible. 'Tell her to keep it,' said the producer.

When the illness had passed and Vivien was recuperating at their home Notley Abbey, David Niven visited England. He says:

'Larry rang me and said that Vivien wanted to see me alone. I went down for dinner and so typically like her, she said, "Now Wivern" [her pet name for him] "tell me everything that happened and don't miss out one single detail. I must know everything". So I told her and she listened quietly to the end.'

After any of her illnesses, with those impeccable manners, Vivien Leigh always wrote a letter to any person to whom she felt she owed an explanation or apology during the period of her illness that she could not remember.

This is not only carrying good manners to the ultimate, but it takes unbelievable courage.

During this illness for the first time in her life Vivien herself began to worry about the future and her mental stability. Each attack had become more severe and it took longer to recover.

'When they say I am well I feel ghastly and when they say I am unwell I feel wonderful,' she told a friend.

But such was her extraordinary resilience that in July, four months later, after resting in the country, she was back in London glowingly healthy and planning to work again. At a cocktail party held at Hugh ('Binkie') Beaumont's she was at her gayest and quipped:

'I would like to forget all about the last four months but unfortunately it is not the kind of thing that one forgets easily. As for *Elephant Walk* you mustn't blame the elephants. Anyway my illness hasn't made the slightest difference. I smoke and drink as before.'

At this party it was announced that in partnership with Laurence Olivier, H M Tennent's would present the pair in *The Sleeping Princess*, written specially for the Oliviers by Terence Rattigan who described it as 'an occasional fairy story'.

During rehearsals friends worried in case Vivien could not stand up to the strain. Instead she bloomed. Her only concession to her illness was that she insisted that the heating in the theatre was turned up full.

'Oh it is so wonderful to be back,' she purred, and everyone warmed to make it a happy production. In her rôle as Elaine Dagenham, a flirty American chorus girl who invades a fictitious Carpathian Embassy in London in 1911 and throws a Balkan prince (Laurence Olivier) into a tizz, Vivien was delicious. It was stuff that dreams are made of when she passes out after a vodka session with the Duke and three flunkies pick her up and carry her out.

In the demure, dainty white dress Roger Furze designed

for her ('I kept it simple because I wanted people to look at Vivien and not the dress') and a blonde wig with frivolous curls on her cheeks she looked like one of those expensive pink and white porcelain dolls that came from Germany.

Due to Vivien's illness the play opened in Manchester in September 1953, four months overdue, but the box office was happy. It was a complete sell-out for the week. On the opening night £12,000 was netted for charity. Her dressing room was filled entirely with white flowers except a posy of pink and white roses from Laurence Olivier.

When the Oliviers entered the restaurant of the Midland Hotel for supper after the performance the packed room stood and applauded. It was not only a salute to a dazzlingly beautiful woman but to her comeback so soon after her illness.

By the time the play moved south, London was willing and ready. For the opening at the Phoenix three ambassadors were present (France, Sweden and Brazil), the Duff Coopers, Douglas Fairbanks, Somerset Maugham, Terence Rattigan brought his mother, John Mills and Stewart Grainger, to name a few celebrities. Vivien could hardly move in her dressing room it was so swamped with flowers.

As Elizabeth Frank wrote next day: 'Two seconds after the curtain rose on the blue and pink Edwardian set the double doors were thrown open and there she was – a girl of about seventeen in a white dress and curly blonde hair as gay and carefree as a prize kitten. And did the audience coo over her.'

The cynical London critics were like men bewitched. As Cecil Wilson wrote:

'Miss Leigh is the most disarming little demon who ever upset a royal applecart. She minces round the legation in a wide-eyed daze of innocence and guile and carries her American accent with a practised ease. It is the teasing

sing-song accent of Blanche du Bois suddenly aware that all that neurotic nonsense was only a nightmare.'

After the opening performance Terence Rattigan gave a party at his Eaton Square penthouse to celebrate Vivien's fortieth birthday and welcome her back. First to arrive was Somerset Maugham and first to leave was Somerset Maugham. John Mills led the singing of *Happy Birthday* and the party went on until 4.30 am. When the papers arrived with their ecstatic reviews about the Oliviers, Noël Coward turned to Terence Rattigan and said: 'You see the Oliviers have ruined your play just as the Lunts ruined mine.'

Marriage Under Pressure

THE BEGINNING AND the end of the Oliviers' marriage was mainly due to their passionate dedication to their acting careers. When two people care deeply for each other it is seldom that their marriage can survive long separations forced by their personal ambitions.

There was another reason too – Vivien Leigh's difficult periods of ill-health – manic depression – over which she had little control. Had she taken the advice of her friends and doctors to take life gently, even this may have been overcome. But during these periods she became extraordinarily difficult for anyone to advise.

In the early days of Laurence Olivier's marriage to Vivien Leigh, when their professional lives were closely knit, they were separated as seldom as possible. Theirs was an intense love. This hatred of being apart was, as shown earlier, responsible for Vivien Leigh being tested for the part of Scarlett in *Gone With the Wind*. On the spur of the moment she went to Hollywood for five days to be with Laurence Olivier who was going through a difficult period. During this time she was tested for 'Scarlett' and secured the part.

As their professional lives broadened they found that it was not always possible to appear in the same plays together. The part was either right for Olivier and wrong for Vivien or right for Vivien and wrong for Olivier. They spent all their spare time reading through plays trying to find scripts which were suitable for them both. But it was not easy. Vivien's exotic beauty, and the fact that she always looked twenty years younger than her years, was no doubt a great help in her career, but it also was a hindrance towards playing in some of the great classics which suited Olivier.

Their close friends, the Lunts, had managed to stay acting together in America but their range was limited compared with the Oliviers and their acting talent so interwoven that this was an exceptional case.

Elizabeth Taylor and Richard Burton seem to have found the answer of working together but again their marriage is relatively new and only time will tell whether 'togetherness' wins over personal ambition.

During the mid-fifties there had been continual rumours that the Oliviers' marriage was not working out. But any marriage between two famous people, which is subjected to the full blaze of the Press, has the indignity of suffering from over-exposure.

From 1957 onwards the rumours had been stronger than ever before. Whatever their private feelings were on the matter neither Vivien Leigh nor Laurence Olivier acknowledged their difficulties publicly. They gave few interviews and shunned most gossip writers except the trusted few in the inner circle. They were determined to keep their personal feelings as remote as possible from their professional lives and therefore from the general public.

During the next two years, because of their acting commitments, they were together less and less. Friends began to notice, too, that when they were together at Notley Abbey there were often signs of tension and friction. Just small insignificant straws that in any other marriage may not have been important. But with the Oliviers it was different. Sadly in the glory of their high octane years they seemed to grow further apart.

Vivien Leigh was a gregarious collector of people. She loved to swamp her life with friends, with parties, with gaiety. She hated being alone and rationed herself to a few hours sleep a night.

Sir Laurence needed peace and time to regenerate the immense energy he used up in his theatre work. Parties bored him. He liked their theatrical friends a few at a time, when he could really talk about the things in the theatre that mattered to him. He enjoyed simple things. He preferred the 'hash' or steak and kidney pudding that the staff ate to the exotic, expensive foods Vivien chose for themselves and their friends. And he needed sleep. Lots of it.

One friend recalling a weekend party at Notley says:

'The house was full of guests and we had had a marvellous lunch. Vivien was in one of her provoking moods and for no reason at all began shouting at Larry in an uncontrollable rage from one end of the lunch table to the other. None of us knew where to look. The party broke up. I went to my room wondering what the next step would be. Surely it was the end of the weekend. I would pack and then make some excuse about getting back to London. All the other guests seemed to disappear too. Larry took himself off for a solitary walk and Vivien went to her bedroom.

'When I sneaked out of my room at about 6 pm to try to get a car to take me to the station, there was Vivien looking simply marvellous.

' "But darling, you can't go now. Look (pointing to the drive and two cars that were arriving) I've asked the so-and-so's and so-and-so's to dinner." Hearing us, the rest of the guests began to emerge sheepishly from their rooms.

'When Larry returned to the house there was yet another party in full swing.'

The show must go on. . . .

It was distressing to everyone around because not only was theirs one of the great romances of the twentieth-century theatre, but they had publicly and privately worked hard to keep alive the illusion of a great love story.

'Had they been lesser people we may have been able to do more. But here were two very intelligent and strong-willed people and it was difficult for anyone to advise them,' a friend recalls.

'We all hoped that somehow even if there was a separation that this would be temporary and in time they could find a way to live together again.

'Loving and admiring them both as we all did we could only hope that given time and no pressure they would sort it out as many other middle-aged couples have done before. It was inconceivable that Vivien and Larry should part.'

If Vivien Leigh had been prepared to slip into semi-retirement and only act occasionally, when a really irresistible part was available, there was a possibility that it could have worked out. But she had to work consistently and intensely to live, because work was her life. She became bored, depressed and difficult during the time she was not working. Even her holidays were trimmed into short spells so that she could begin work again as soon as possible.

As writer David York says:

'Simple continuous happiness was not in her nature. For her the moments of joy and true satisfaction – widely spaced and deeply treasured – were almost all associated with the peaks of her career and how she worked to reach them.

'Between times, when she walked in the valleys of ordinary existence, she seemed strangely remote and withdrawn, almost quietly sad.'

The mental breakdowns that Vivien Leigh suffered from always reached their peak when she was under severe strain of overwork. This awesome energy that she generated while assimilating a new part seemed to burn her up until her nerves would suddenly snap.

As one Hollywood director says: 'I always think of the films as being especially suitable for Vivien because of her health and temperament. You could see the signs of strain beginning and then one day the real danger. She stayed up late, surrounding herself with people, and she drank more than she normally did. Then one day she would snap. In a film it could be tempered and, because of her supreme professionalism, she was able to control herself. But in the theatre once the play was running dear Vivi got bored, just bored. And that's when the trouble began.'

There had been signs before but it was during the filming of *Elephant Walk* in Ceylon in 1953 that her mental illness reached its peak, forcing her to leave the film and return to England. And now, over the years, it recurred regularly every time she overtaxed her strength.

During these periods she suffered acute depression and unhappiness. Treatment and complete rest were the only remedy. It was due to her own indomitable will-power that she was able to overcome these periods. Lesser women would not.

'I have been carried back from America on a stretcher so many times because I have been ill or had a nervous breakdown that I am always being told I ought to rest,' she said. 'I would like to rest and particularly to wonder . . . but the only time I have to wonder is when I am ill and I don't really feel like it then.'

By 1959 it had become common talk, in the theatrical worlds of London and New York, that in fact the marriage was finished.

'Every marriage has its ups and downs. This marriage is not an exception,' said Vivien Leigh when discussing the rumours to a reporter. 'It is causing comment only because we are famous.'

When asked point blank if there was going to be an official separation, she answered:

'I won't say no and I won't say yes.'

Sir Laurence was more explicit. Choosing his words very carefully, he said:

'Neither of us knows what the outcome will be. Many marriages have gone through bad times without ending in disaster. Vivien and I want to work things out privately.'

Vivien Leigh was rehearsing in London for *Look After Lulu* and going to Notley Abbey for weekends. Laurence Olivier was at Stratford rehearsing *Coriolanus*.

Godfrey Winn was a weekend house guest at the time and later related that he and Vivien walked in the garden after dinner among the sweetly scented tobacco plants. Vivien Leigh looked beautiful in white chiffon. She told him that she was expecting a phone call after the performance.

As they walked and talked they both had one ear listening for the telephone.

But the call never came.

Late in the evening Godfrey Winn went to bed and Vivien stayed downstairs alone until the early hours of the morning.

'In the morning nothing was said or ever afterwards. She would never allow any of her friends to criticise Laurence Olivier in her presence. Nor did she ever reproach him.'

On the opening night of *Look After Lulu* at the Royal Court Theatre on 29th July, Laurence Olivier was in the stalls and he and Vivien left the theatre arm in arm. To the fans at the stage door it was just like it had always been.

And so the next few months went by.

In the spirit of their new independence the Oliviers decided to spend Christmas apart. Laurence Olivier was planning to go to America and Vivien was going to stay with Noël Coward at his house in Switzerland. He had arranged a series of gay parties as an antidote to the separation rumours.

A week before in a London hospital, Ernest Hartley, Vivien Leigh's father, died. This quiet, unassuming gentleman had always kept himself in the background of the life of both his wife and daughter. But he was immensely proud of the success of Vivien and through the years had kept a scrapbook of her triumphs. When friends called it was the first thing he showed them.

Mrs Hartley, a strong personality and great beauty from whom Vivien had inherited her looks, was involved in her daughter's life in that she had taken so much of the responsibility of bringing up her grand-daughter Suzanne. She was also one of Vivien's staunchest supporters especially during the time of her breakdowns.

Besides, they had a very common bond. They had both worked hard to create the image of Vivien Leigh.

It was therefore only natural that Vivien cancelled her trip and decided to stay in London to be near her mother.

Divorce

Look After Lulu, Noël Coward's play, based on a farce by Georges Feydeau, was not the success that had been hoped for, and received mixed notices. Vivien Leigh played the rôle of Lulu D'Arville and was generally highly praised by the critics, both for her timeless beauty and her adept handling of the part.

The *Sunday Times* critic, whilst lamenting Coward's restrained adaptation of Feydeau's fast-moving farce, qualified his criticism by saying: 'If *Look After Lulu* is only half a success, the reasons are more than complimentary The trouble is that Mr Noël Coward is too witty and Miss Vivien Leigh too beautiful. For the kind of play that *Look After Lulu* is, beauty and wit are as unnecessary as a peach melba at the North Pole.' He ended his criticism by observing that 'In her costume of the second act, Miss Leigh does not, as Feydeau intended, look ridiculous, absurd, grotesque. On the contrary, she looks ravishing, for she cannot look anything else. She moves with extreme grace, and the timing and intelligence of her performance are perfect.'

The play ran for sixteen weeks before closing. As soon as it finished – April 1960 – Vivien Leigh went to New York with Mary Ure in a revival of the great success *Duel of Angels*.

This restlessness and dynamic energy drove her on to work – often at ill-advised times.

Once again the Oliviers were going their lives alone. Whether in fact Vivien Leigh deliberately planned the next

Shakespeare, with Sir Laurence: (*left*) as Lady Macbeth at Stratford-on-Avon in 1955 and (*below*) with Sir Laurence in a Paris production of *Titus Andronicus* at the Theatre Sarah Bernhardt in 1957.

Central Press

From the family albums:
(*right*) with her daughter,
Suzanne, and Miss Leigh's
former husband, Leigh Holman,
on holiday in Italy in 1957.
At the age of forty-five Lady
Olivier became a grandmother
and she is shown (*below*) with
her daughter and her son-in-
law, Mr Robin Farrington, with
the baby – Neville Leigh – in
her arms.

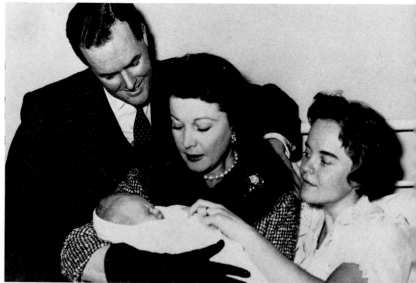

UPI

Nearly three years later Neville
Leigh is quite the young man
and is shown (*right*) at Miss
Leigh's side as she attends to
her make-up during a break in
the filming of *The Roman
Spring of Mrs Stone*.

Camera Press

few months' separation in order to give them both time to think, is something that she did not even discuss with her closest friends. 'Vivien could be very withdrawn when it came to her personal feelings.'

Talking at the time to David Lewin, the English film critic and friend, Vivien Leigh said:

'For a couple of years we have lived much of our lives apart and when I have been working in one country Larry has usually been somewhere else.'

To another friend she commented:

'I do not think that marriage is a thing to be entered into lightly or ended. My play in New York is finishing on 4th June and Larry ends his season in London, too. I have not really very much to come back home for so I have written to Larry that he comes to meet me in New York or anywhere else he may decide. Then we can talk and work things out. I love Larry, but we must decide on something ... we can't let this go on as it is.'

In New York Vivien Leigh drew her usual chic first-night audience when she opened in *The Duel of Angels*, the strong-meat play by André Giradoux.

No one knew the back stage drama that was taking place as the audience filed into their seats. Since her arrival from London, Vivien had been having daily shock treatment.

On the opening night she was distraught. She wept uncontrollably and refused to go on the stage. The small cast, who were intimate friends, discussed what to do, then Peter Wyngarde, her co-star both in London and New York, gently pushed her on stage, tears still falling and her mascara blurred on her cheeks.

'Vivien gave the best performance ever. She was so marvellous that I came out of my part and watched her. I have never seen such brilliant acting,' says Wyngarde.

All during the New York run Vivien Leigh had shock

treatment in the morning and played in the theatre every night. It was an incredible display of bravery and professionalism.

Another poignant account of this period comes from London journalist, Rex North. He had known Vivien Leigh for many years and liked and admired her.

He had called to see her in her dressing room at the theatre.

'There was a bowl of red roses on her table (at the moment Vivien buys them for herself) and six photos of Laurence Olivier.

' "Darling, darling, so nice to see you," she said. "Have a drink or don't. Stand up or sit down. Do anything you like, providing you talk to me while I put a face on for the show. God, I must have the oldest face in the world."

' "Viv," I said, "Viv, do sit down for a second because in thirty-five minutes the curtain goes up and before that you and I have important things to discuss."

'The actress carried on with her performance for an audience of one:

' "Darling, darling, ask me anything, anything."

' "Vivien," I said, "Vivien is it true that you and Larry are going to divorce?"

'The actress vanished, the woman appeared. When I asked the question, Vivien was dabbing green paint on her eyes and then she shifted her stare a fraction to look at my reflection as I sat behind her.

'Then . . . and this I will never forget . . . one tear, a big, bulb of a tear, lingered on her left eyelid and dropped on her pink silk dressing gown.

'Then Vivien Leigh became all woman. She cried and cried.

' "Vivien let's stop fencing with each other. You and Larry are one of the most respected husband-and-wife teams in Britain. But wherever I go in New York, rumours say that there is a divorce action in the offing. . . . In fact, one of them told me last night that the trouble is that you two can't be happy together, or apart from each other. Is it or is it not true that you are parting from Larry for good?"

' "I hope it isn't true," said Vivien – and I swear that she has never spoken a line with more depth and sincerity in the whole of her professional life.

' "About the same time as we come off I think Larry will be free."

' "I have worked it out that we may be able to meet about 4th June. We are apart now, but I feel and hope that if we meet again everything could be all right.

' "Rex, I do hope that I am right. I must. I must be right. . . ."

' "I don't want to meet Larry in England," said Vivien. "Wrong atmosphere. Somewhere abroad. Somewhere wonderful. We must not go on like this. Wish me – us – luck." '

Knowing Vivien Leigh's reserve it is amazing that she willingly opened her heart to 4,500,000 of Rex North's newspaper readers. The only explanation after a period of eight years is that in fact it was a woman fighting for something that she cared desperately about. She was not to know what lay ahead, because life is not as simple as that. There was no crystal ball. Here was a proud, cosseted beauty with the world at her feet. She had never known a real setback in her life. Somehow she would handle this, too.

'I learnt so much from Vivien both as an actress and as a woman,' says Mary Ure who was playing opposite her in *Duel of Angels*. 'She was such a wonderful person.'

Robert Helpmann who directed the play wanted Peter

Wyngarde to wear tight black riding breeches instead of the loose white ones he had worn in London, and to dispense with a jock strap.

When Vivien saw the result she quipped: 'If you come on without a jock strap the audience isn't going to look at you or me or anything else. On with your jock strap, dear!'

Ill as she was and personally unhappy Vivien was determined that the tour would be a gay one for the rest of the company. In Hollywood all the stars and friends turned up on the opening night. The John Mills brought Hayley, then a young teenager, much against the wishes of her studio bosses in Disney.

Next morning Mrs Mills (Mary Hayley Bell) received something like thirty telegrams of protest from various women's organisations – the Daughters of This and That – all protesting that Hayley, the epitome of a young virgin, should be allowed to see such a degenerate play.

'Mary Hayley Bell was in a terrible state until she found out that they had all been sent by Vivien,' says Wyngarde.

Back in London, Sir Laurence Olivier had made a fresh milestone for his interpretation of the seedy song-and-dance Archie Rice in John Osborne's *The Entertainer*. In one of those audacious surprises, with which he likes to punctuate his career, he had succeeded in giving yet another brilliant performance.

For his leading lady he had chosen a relatively unknown actress called Joan Plowright. Daughter of a newspaper editor in Scunthorpe, North Lincolnshire, she had made a considerable acting career including playing a ship-boy of eight in the film *Moby Dick*. As a 'heavyweight fairy' with the Old Vic Company touring South Africa she had fallen in love with a young actor Roger Gage whom she later married.

In New York, Vivien Leigh knew how much Laurence

Olivier admired Joan Plowright's integrity as an actress. He had written how delighted he was to have her in the cast. But she did not know of the gossip in London of the unexpected friendship that had developed between the fifty-three-year-old actor and the thirty-one-year-old actress.

Like many other wives she was to be among the last to realise.

It has happened before and it will happen again. A man deprived of any real marriage for several years finds himself in a vacuum. Whether he knows it himself or not he is, inside, lonely and hurt and vulnerable.

Joan Plowright happened to be in Olivier's orbit at the right moment. Her own marriage had begun to drift.

Why did nobody warn Vivien Leigh that in fact the marriage was now in serious danger? Simply because under any circumstances it is a very difficult thing to do and all her zealous friends were anxious to shield her from any unpleasantness that might bring on one of her nervous depressions. Besides, they still desperately hoped that even now the marriage might be saved.

In the beginning of June, Vivien Leigh flew to England to talk with her husband. Her arrival filled in any blanks there might have been. Now she knew everything. That Sir Laurence wanted a divorce so that he could marry Joan Plowright.

It was a shattering experience for Vivien Leigh. For the first time in her life since she was a child she had not got what she wanted. She was completely bewildered.

She filled in those desperate days going to familiar places with familiar faces. One day she and Mrs John Mills made a sentimental return visit into Buckinghamshire to visit Notley Abbey again. It was here that the Oliviers had spent their most glamorous days together as the first couple of the British stage. Their weekend parties were legendary.

Notley had been sold to Canadian writer Arnold Swanson, who was delighted to accompany the distinguished Lady Olivier over her former home, and show her the brand new kitchen he had installed.

'She didn't say very much,' he commented afterwards. 'But just looked very sad as she walked from room to room.'

The massive rose garden which had been her joy had been bulldozed up for a swimming pool but not yet completed. Just mounds of earth where every weekend in the summer she had picked trugfuls of roses.

Everywhere she looked had memories – the trees Laurence Olivier liked to prune, the quiet cloisters where they often walked before dinner, the view of the gentle river Thame and the sweep of rolling Buckinghamshire country.

After the divorce it was one of the great regrets of Vivien Leigh's life that in fact they had sold Notley Abbey which was the only real home she ever loved. But at the time it seemed too filled with poignant memories.

It seems unbelievable that a sophisticated woman like Vivien Leigh would resort to such a romantic, hurtful pilgrimage. But a proud, sensitive beauty who sees her whole world tumbling round her knows no reason.

Any of Vivien Leigh's strange behaviour in the next month must be viewed with tolerance. Her fragile nerves, shock, and deep hurt compelled her to actions she may not have taken otherwise.

After visiting Notley, Vivien Leigh had planned to go to the theatre and see Laurence Olivier in his new play *Rhinoceros*, but her friends persuaded her that while the heat of the Press was on it would be better for them both if she stayed away.

Instead, she went with a party of friends – Noël Coward, the John Mills, Robert Helpmann and Michael Benthall – to see Alec Guinness in *Ross* at the Haymarket. She left by the side door saying she was tired and not feeling very well.

There was not a friend who did not want to rush to her side. Just as she herself had given unstinted friendship all her life, now they wanted to be near and protect her.

On 19th June Sir Laurence and Lady Olivier met for one brief hour.

At 1 pm he arrived at the Eaton Square flat driving his blue Jaguar. One hour later he drove off. Just ten minutes passed and Lady Olivier, unsmiling, took a taxi and went to see her close friend and dressmaker, Victor Stiebel.

She was completely shattered and numb. She could not – and never did over the years ahead – believe that Laurence Olivier would leave her. She trusted that the bond between them was so strong that somehow it could survive anything – even if the conditions were to her making.

With dignity she was to later remark that Sir Laurence's marriage to Joan Plowright was only a sequel to the end of the marriage and not the cause.

'Basically it was work that broke it up,' she explained.

On the following day Vivien Leigh flew back to America, and on arrival announced to a stunned New York Press that Laurence Olivier had asked her for a divorce so that he could marry Joan Plowright.

By her direct action any possible hope of a reconciliation in the marriage had been irredeemably shattered.

Six months later in the London Courts, before Judge Ifor Lloyd on 2nd December, Vivien Leigh was granted a divorce from Sir Laurence Olivier on the grounds of his adultery with Miss Joan Plowright.

As she stood up to give evidence wearing a red and black check suit and looking pale, there was an air of tragedy about this small figure. When she spoke, in a low husky voice, tears began to roll down her cheeks. She wiped them away delicately with the tips of her gloved fingers.

She left the court with a friend, actor Jack Merivale, who drove her away in her own pale blue Rolls-Royce. She sat in the back seat, looking straight ahead and regardless of the photographers who surged round the car. Together they went to Henley-on-Thames where Merivale's stepmother, Gladys Cooper, lived.

Both Joan Plowright and Laurence Olivier were not present in court as they were in America.

In the same court and because of the same adultery, Joan Plowright's husband, actor Roger Gage, was granted a decree nisi against his wife.

When everything was ultimately finalised Vivien Leigh said:

'If I were really and truly given the chance to live my life all over again, I would be certain of only two things. One is that at an early age I would become an actress. The other is that at a not much later age I should marry Laurence Olivier – and do the proposing myself if necessary. I would want to do everything again, except the last few months.

'I miss Larry terribly. If you live with a man for twenty-five years you don't suddenly stop missing him.'

Tomorrow . . .

'TOMORROW IS ANOTHER day. For me tomorrow will always be exciting – and worth fighting for,' Scarlett O'Hara said.

When she was making *Gone With the Wind* these words impressed Vivien who frequently quoted them as a guide in her own life.

Three days after her divorce from Sir Laurence Olivier in December 1960 she began a new life by giving a party for forty friends at her Eaton Square flat. Among them was actor John ('Jack') Merivale who had been her companion over the last few months.

It was Jack Merivale, laden with coats and hand luggage, who shepherded her through the Customs at Cherbourg a few months before when she was returning to England for the divorce.

He was there to soothe her when the Customs at Cherbourg tried to impound her Renoir (valued at £5,000). Indignantly she had said to the bewildered Customs:

'I have had it for five years and I never travel without it.' Then Jack took over.

It was also Jack Merivale who handled her by the arm from the court after the divorce and taking the wheel of her Rolls-Royce dodged Press photographers like a seasoned rally driver.

Merivale's friendship with the Oliviers stretched back over twenty-five years. He had acted in the ill-fated production of *Romeo and Juliet* on Broadway in 1940.

His step-mother, Gladys Cooper, and step-brother John

Buckmaster, had been friends of Vivien Leigh's for many years. His father, Philip Merivale, was the first Professor Higgins to act in *Pygmalion* on Broadway.

Tall, bearded Jack Merivale with his cut-glass Guardee looks is reminiscent of Peter Townsend. He was born in Canada but educated at Rugby and Oxford. It was while he was at Oxford, playing in the Oxford University Dramatic Society, that he decided to give up studying and take up acting as a full-time career studying first with the Old Vic.

During the war he served with the Canadian Air Force and in 1941 married actress Jan Sterling.

The fact that Merivale, with his looks, has never emerged as a star actor is probably due to innate shyness in being the son of famous parents.

It is regrettable that probably his best performance in *La Dame aux Camelias*, as produced by the Old Vic on Vivien Leigh's last tour of Australia, was never seen on the London stage. It was the same rôle that John Gilbert had played with Garbo in the film version. And the same situation that both young actors were devoted to their leading ladies.

At her *après-divorce* party, he was among the many friends present. Vivien had once said: 'I need a man in my life. To be alone is nothing.'

'Jack was very good for Vivien,' an onlooker at the party said. 'It was Jack who always carried everything and yet remained quietly in the background when Vivien was getting her star treatment. During the last months of her illness Jack was simply wonderful.'

In April 1961, Lady Olivier and Jack Merivale went to stay as the guests of Mr and Mrs Chester Martin in Montego Bay, in Jamaica. Although she naturally retained the name of Vivien Leigh in the theatre in her private life she remained

Vivien, Lady Olivier, and always used her title to domestic or hotel staff.

They had intended to stay only seven days but in the end stretched it out to three weeks, moving to the Arnos Vale Hotel in Tobago.

Here again they were harassed by reporters. When asked about marriage rumours (of which the whole of Jamaica was buzzing) Vivien Leigh parried provocatively:

'Those rumours are just not true. But then those kind of rumours never are, are they?'

When a persistent reporter pressed further:

'Do you plan to marry Mr Merivale before the coming Far East tour of the Old Vic?' she answered:

'That's private.'

Back in London the lower strata of the professional acquaintances thought a marriage was possible, but the small, inner ring knew that she had no intention of marrying anyone – not yet, anyway.

In her own sad, illogical way she still regarded herself as the wife of Laurence Olivier.

During this romantic holiday, when they swam from the golden beaches by day and danced under a star-strewn sky at night, Vivien Leigh had one upsetting experience.

She was robbed of her handbag containing £100, her passport, a sapphire ring and two gold cigarette lighters valued at £500. One was the lighter in the shape of a star that David Selznick had given her as a memento of Scarlett.

Looking happier and healthier than she had for months Vivien Leigh returned from the Bahamas at the end of April. Back to the English spring, which she always loved so much, and a new country house.

Despite her conventional upbringing Vivien Leigh was a gypsy at heart – continually restless and moving from country to country. She loved everything about travelling –

shopping wherever she was, dropping in on old friends, buying up amusing bric-à-brac to ship back. She could never settle for long.

She said that 'serendipity' was her favourite hobby and this she defined as 'the gift of finding valuable things in unexpected places by sheer luck'.

While she was married to Laurence Olivier and chatelaine of Notley Abbey and Durham Cottage in Chelsea, she once said that she felt that the really dedicated actor or actress should shed their domestic and material responsibilities and travel the world like jet-age strolling players.

But this she could not bring herself to do. She was sufficiently bourgeois to care about roots. She always maintained well-run established houses for herself, her friends and her cats.

Whenever she stayed in America for any length of time it was never the expensive hotel suite that attracted her. She immediately found an apartment where she would install herself with staff and then proceed to fill it with flowers and friends. It is a most lovable streak in this complicated woman's nature. At one period she had sixteen Siamese cats, all adored by her, scattered round the various houses and flats which she had at the time.

But no matter how many months of the year she was away from England come the spring, like a homing white dove she came back. Back to her Vivien-world of English garden flowers, snuff boxes, signed photos from friends, books, bundles of old letters that she always kept, her beloved china collection, paintings she treasured, boxes of theatre programmes, big collection of perfumes and her own monogrammed linen.

Though she loved America and regarded it as her second home – 'New York, Chicago, Denver, they give me vitality' – in the end it was in the English countryside that she recuperated her health and energy.

Since Notley Abbey had been sold she had been looking for a new country house.

This she found in Tickeridge Mill, an elegant five-bedroomed Queen Anne mill house at Uckfield in Sussex which had once been owned by Lord Snowdon's father, the late Mr Ronald Armstrong Jones. Hidden in a valley of the river Uck it was set in ninety acres of woodlands and garden and would provide the privacy she wanted.

There was a lake with an outfall to the mill pond and a stream stocked with trout. Vivien had always said that she was happiest when she was within distance of water.

An interior decorator had been engaged to put the house in order for although she enjoyed creating her own atmosphere it was also a question of time. And of this Vivien Leigh never seemed to have enough. Though she only allowed herself five or six hours' sleep a day there was still not enough time left to do all the things she wanted to do.

But at no time could one say that her house had been done by so-and-so. She left her own indelible print on each house by the placing of objects in her own way and the choice of her own colours.

A special place was found for the two Oscars she had won in her film life. The first one for the part of 'Scarlett' in *Gone With the Wind* was used as door-stop in the drawing room and the one for Blanche in *A Streetcar Named Desire* was positioned in the downstairs lavatory.

In the dining room they hung the unfinished portrait of Vivien Leigh by Augustus John. What promised to be the most revealing of the fifteen attempts by artists to capture her elusive beauty was never finished. John preferred rum and ruminations and Vivien got bored.

Moving-in day at Tickeridge Mill was fun. In a denim skirt, cotton shirt and peasant headscarf Vivien was there to supervise the unpacking of the crates. Jack Merivale helped her and it was champagne all round for the removal men.

In the village of Uckfield there was curiosity, too, among the older inhabitants. Will she be stand-offish or mix and be one of us? they asked.

Vivien Leigh spent the spring at Uckfield, each day filled with new surprises in the garden. There were new plants, rose bushes and trees to be ordered.

'To buy a house when everything is asleep and watch the garden wake is a marvellous experience,' she said. She frequently took weekend guests to the *Crown Inn* where everyone joined in.

'She could talk with a duke or a dustman. It was all the same to her. We all loved her,' is how Mrs Freda Lewis, the licensee at the time, remembers her.

On Saturday mornings it was like a club with everyone dropping in. Vivien just loved talking to people and used to begin chatting with the old men in the bar. If they were drinking something different, like barley wine for instance, she would always ask if she could taste it. They didn't have any idea who she was and she didn't care.

Poor Mrs Stone

WHENEVER VIVIEN LEIGH was asked by the Press why she had done a particular thing or taken a certain step, she invariably answered, 'Because it was expedient.' It was a neat, surgical way of explaining nothing.

'It was expedient' that she be out of England during the spring of 1961. The memory of her divorce was still poignant and the theatre scene was too constraining for two Lady Oliviers at that moment.

Work and a spell abroad seemed the antidote to her present sadness. With her fixed opinions she did not like the original short story *The Roman Spring of Mrs Stone*, and when Tennessee Williams approached her to make the film, she refused. But now with time to fill in, and with the possibility of filming in Italy during the early spring, she agreed. It was six years since she had made her last film.

'I read the script again,' Vivien Leigh said on accepting the rôle, 'and decided I wanted to do it. There were certain basic changes in the character of Mrs Stone and certain explanations why her life began to drift that made me change my mind about doing it.'

Could it have also been that her recent experience had made her more tolerant and understanding of lonely, rich beauties?

It was one of Vivien Leigh's most endearing and obstinate traits that she would never accept a part unless she herself understood it. She always quoted that it was the actor's responsibility 'to assimilate the author's interpretation and stick to it'. But in her case she had first to be convinced that the author's way was in fact her own. With the alterations to the script of *Mrs Stone* she now felt that she understood the stringent truth of this theme on the fading beauty and power of an ageing woman.

The studio had rented a superb flat for her in Rome. Before signing the contract she had stipulated that the major part of her wardrobe was to be chosen by her and designed by Balmain. In fact, of the thirty costume changes sixteen came from Paris.

To cut down time, the dresses were made on the plastic dummy that Balmain kept of her figure and it was only at the end that she spent days in the Paris fitting rooms until every dress was absolutely perfect. She was as meticulous about her stage clothes and accessories as those she wore in private life.

For seven weeks a skeleton unit had been working in Rome choosing location shots. Just a few days before the entire unit were to fly to Rome the Italian Minister for Tourism and Spectacle notified producer Louis de Rochemont that the Italian Government would not allow the unit in.

The explanation given was that the screenplay, which had been submitted for approval many months before, contained material defamatory to Italy as it showed Rome as a corrupt city. Italian society was still smarting from the revelations of *La Dolce Vita*.

A lightning switch was made so that work could begin at the Associated British Studios at Elstree. Shooting began on the interior scenes in Mrs Stone's luxurious flat which was meant to be located near the Spanish Steps in Rome and production designer Roger Furze had the strenuous task of preparing one of the largest 'street' scenes ever built in a British studio at record speed. Complete with shops, restaurants, banks, garages, a beauty salon and barber's shop and hotel the street covered the entire area of Stage 4

The beginning, and the
beginning of the end. Twenty
years separate these two
photographs. The earlier
picture (*above*), taken in
December 1939, shows Vivien
Leigh and Laurence Olivier at
the Atlanta, Georgia, première
of *Gone With the Wind*.

(*Left*) Vivien Leigh with Sir
Laurence in December 1959,
less than a year before their
divorce.

In 1941, after their marriage, Laurence Olivier and Vivien Leigh played their part in the war effort, as shown above where they are serving tea to British soldiers.

Two years later Vivien Leigh appeared with John Gielgud i *The Doctor's Dilemma* at London's Haymarket Theatre. They are shown (*left*) in Miss Leigh's dressing room.

at Elstree. The British Fiat Company even produced left-hand drive Italian taxis and cars to fill the street.

It was as if from the unnerving beginning of the film, the whole company were determined that the unit would be a happy one. If she was annoyed or disappointed at not going to Rome, Vivien Leigh never showed it on the set. 'From the pre-production party to the final shot,' says cameraman Harry Waxman, 'I never saw her cross.'

The studio did everything to compensate and make Vivien happy. It found a small uncredited part for Jack Merivale and gave her the usual star-treatment dressing room, but she had also asked for a caravan on the set. This was newly decorated in pale green chintz from curtains to chaise longue and Vivien moved in her pictures, books, flowers, photos and Siamese cats.

'It was extraordinary, just an ordinary caravan outside but inside she had made it into a small sitting room. To be asked there was considered a great honour. I have worked with many top stars but none of them did this. It was absolutely charming,' says Bob Webb, publicist on the film.

She always looked attractive, too. In the early morning when many stars arrive at the studio bleary-eyed, ghostly without make-up, wearing crumpled slacks, dark glasses, some grotesque head covering and gasping for black coffee, Vivien was different. She was immaculate and could have been going to a point-to-point meeting or a lunch date at the Ivy. Instead of the tired towelling wraps or make-up spattered housecoats that one usually sees on a set, Vivien always wore perfectly tailored pure silk cut like a man's dressing gown – and looked ravishing.

Many of her friends thought that with her transparently pale, fine skin her face had more real beauty when she did not wear make-up.

In Hollywood it may have been different but in England Vivien Leigh inspired a special dignity even on the set.

'We all would have done anything for her but apart from the director and co-actors we always addressed her as Miss Leigh. We daren't call her Vivien. She had that kind of stature,' says Bob Webb. 'It wasn't that she was in any way demanding – far from it. She would sit alone on the set in any chair she could find and she never asked for a special big chair like some of them. One day I plucked up courage to sit beside her and she told me she had been to see François Trufaut's *Four Hundred Blows* the night before. She was so excited about it and explained that it was a completely new concept of picture making:

' "Oh how I wish they'd offer me a part in one of these new-wave pictures," she remarked sadly.'

It was inevitable but here was the actress, then rated as the biggest box office attraction in the world, desperately wanting to be included in the new Continental experimental film world that she knew was bypassing her. She resented being typed even although in latter years she had only herself to blame for it.

The laconic film crew on the set, even now, years later, rhapsodise about her professionalism. There was not a detail that missed her. Before the continuity girl could tell her she knew exactly how far a cigarette had burnt down in a shot from the previous day. She understood every camera angle and lights and had a phobia about being late on the set.

She could be tired, deflated, even cross at the delays but the moment the director called 'Vivien . . .' by some inner force she would pull herself together. This tiny, fragile figure seemed to grow as she walked with straight back, head authoritatively poised. Again and again she would deliver her lines with the same pitch, same nuance. Camera crew on all her films were floored: 'She just never fluffed. It is difficult to choose her best take.'

Only once did she show temperament, when everyone was on the set and Warren Beatty, who played her gigolo, was absent. She waited five minutes then stormed into her caravan, saying: 'I'm here. I'm waiting and he's not.'

The explanation was that someone had slipped up and Warren Beatty had not been told he was needed. When he did arrive he was distraught and went to her caravan to apologise. Though the crew described Beatty as 'a wild one' for his nonchalance on the set, in this case he could have blamed an assistant but instead remained quiet. Late on set is one of the cardinal sins of film making where every minute wasted costs so much money.

Warren Beatty himself warmed to Vivien's professionalism. He says that he learnt more from working with her for three months than he did all the time he studied at the various method schools.

It was this kind of concrete advice that a young actor appreciates. During one scene with Vivien, Beatty was asked by the director to comb his hair or some such small personal thing but he refused. He didn't feel it was right for him and played the scene straight.

After it was over, Vivien who had remained silent called him aside:

'You silly boy. That scene should have been yours but you gave it away. Now it is mine.' That is all she said but the message was received.

It was particularly during the love scenes that he realised just why this woman had won two Oscars. There was no chi-chi nonsense about her acting. She had prepared every single movement with algebraic logic that on translation to the screen appeared spontaneous and totally natural.

Her technique was her strength, because she was a master

of it, but it may even have been detrimental because it left no room for that spontaneous spark of brilliance that occasionally lights up a whole scene.

The only other time the crew saw her upset was when a newspaper photographer had smuggled himself into the studio and fastened himself on the spot rail. When he was discovered Vivien Leigh was completely unnerved.

Harry Waxman recalls how Vivien would not be rushed. One day a quick close-up was wanted. 'What is this, a quickie?' she asked acidly as the cameras moved in.

Some actors and actresses prefer to leave it to the director and producer, but every evening Vivien insisted on seeing the rushes and personally checked every still photograph before it went out. When this particular shot came up although everyone else thought it was fine she said in her quiet, ladylike voice:

'I think we can do better. Let's do it again.'

It was her own decisive manner in dealing with a situation and making it quite clear that she resented being hurried.

'But no one minded,' says Waxman. Her criticisms were always valid and sensible.

At the end of the film Vivien Leigh asked for a list of the names of every single person who had worked on the set – from the clapper boy upwards.

On the last day she invited them to all come to her caravan where she had a stack of presents prettily wrapped and addressed in her own handwriting. There was a crate of special export whisky for the director and a golden cigarette case for Warren Beatty. She kissed each one of the ninety people as she gave them the gifts.

'It must have cost her all of £1,000 as they all came from Aspreys. It is usual for director and star to exchange gifts but never for an entire film unit,' says Bob Webb, 'but that was Vivien Leigh.'

When the film was released it got, on the whole, good notices. Some people found that she was unconvincing in the rôle. No gigolo would have left a woman looking as young and beautiful, plus all those dollars.

Later, while Vivien Leigh was touring in Australia, Bob Webb cabled news of the way the critics received it. Back came the following cable: 'Dear Bob, how sweet of you, glad to hear of poor Mrs Stone.'

The last time Vivien had visited Australia in 1948 with an Old Vic Company, it had been a royal procession for her and Laurence Olivier. Now, in May 1961, she was alone, the star on whom the whole tour depended.

This time she knew it was going to be tough as the entire trip had been sold on her name, though associated with the Old Vic Company. She had no illusions that she was not carrying the whole company. It was a perfectly good, solid cast but the actors were virtually unknown in Australia, or in England for that matter.

In grand style she had sent ahead Bernard, her chauffeur, and the Rolls with its VLO number plate. The charges on her excess luggage amounted to £250.

'We pay of course. A star like Miss Leigh has to carry so many dresses,' an Old Vic spokesman explained. Vivien Leigh had *The Times* flown out daily so she could keep up with the crosswords.

Although her luggage was still initialled VLO she insisted on being billed and called Vivien Leigh, both to the company and the general public. The only members of the company who called her 'm'lady' were Bernard and her German maid, Trudi, who was also a confidante and relentless guardian.

The male members of the company had been tricked out by Vivien Leigh in special ties which she had had made and

213

the girls had scarves. On a background of Wedgwood blue, there was a laurel wreath to represent a successful tour. A small white flower embroidered, signified *Lady of the Camellias*, two small angel wings *Duel of Angels* and crossed swords for *Twelfth Night*. Inside the laurel wreath were embroidered the individual monograms of each person. It was the kind of intricate present that she loved to plan.

On arrival, the Australian Press was intrigued by the now beardless Jack Merivale at her side and played up the romantic angle heavily with such headlines as: 'She wears her love for all to see' and 'Will they marry here is the question all Australia is asking.'

To coincide with the arrival, English writer the late Nancy Spain, who claimed to be a close friend of the new Lady Olivier (actress Joan Plowright), had put the readers of the largest Australian women's magazine well in the picture about the break-up of the Olivier marriage.

Whether, in fact, Vivien Leigh ever read the article no one knows but at all press conferences the reporter who was naïve enough to touch on her domestic life got a sharp rebuke. Vivien Leigh was always wary of press interviews and seldom relaxed. She conducted herself with an ice-cold regality to all but the favoured half-dozen writers who had penetrated the 'inner circle' over the years. In her dressing room at every theatre she played there were always photographs of Laurence Olivier, as well as in her hotel bedroom.

The Australian tour was not an unqualified success. There were some valid criticisms.

Vivien Leigh had always wanted to play *La Dame aux Camélias* on the London stage. She wore fabulous gowns (one cloak was made from hundreds of ostrich feathers all taken off their quills and mounted on gauze) and looked breathtaking. But her Marguerita did not convince the critic of *The Listener*. He wrote, 'She's not a great tragic actress and the supreme test of the death scene is beyond her emotional scope. Handkerchiefs were not called for.'

Publicity and tour manager Elizabeth Frank explains: 'From the moment Bobbie [director Robert Helpmann] went back to England one felt the difference. Vivien was lost without someone to guide her. In earlier days she had been used to a nightly post mortem at the end of every performance with Larry telling her what had gone wrong. Except for Bobbie there was no one on this tour who was in the position to tell her anything. I couldn't because it wasn't my place and, anyway, I'm not a professional actress. But this straight criticism is something she lacked and I had to do all sorts of trick things. For instance, when she couldn't be heard. I could tell her, but it had to be wrapped up in the fact that there was something wrong with the acoustics. Bobbie could have said:

' "I can't hear a bloody word you are saying, all that mumble mumble and that typewriter performance." And she would have taken it like a lamb.

'All I could ever say to her was something like: "Something is funny about your wig today, dear", or "Your sword [in *Twelfth Night*] is getting in the way." But I could never say: "I can't hear you in the front row of the stalls."

'I loved her dearly but I often found her absolutely impossible. She was stimulating to work with because she was so disarming. We would have the most appalling rows, I used to just leave the room when she started. You always knew when she was going to have a row with you because she addressed you through the mirror when you went into the dressing room. Then next day there would invariably be either a present or a telephone call to apologise. She could be frightfully intolerant. The best thing was not to say anything to her at all then it usually came out all right. She had a blinding temper and often jumped to conclusions. She had a great thing about people being stupid and not seeing the point whereas, very often, she had not taken the trouble to really find out. On the other hand she was basically kind and generous. She was a pathetic character in many ways. She was like a very brilliant child.

'After Larry had left her she had no one to sharpen her wits on. There were only a few left like Robert Helpmann for instance. Most of the people who surrounded her were inclined to be non-intellectual. I remember seeing Vivien with a French ambassador in one of the parties given us. He was a very brilliant man, and she was absolutely transformed conversing with him in her very beautiful French about art, literature and so on. Also there was a conductor who was on tour in South America. He was famous on the Continent and the same thing happened then. She was very happy talking to him. But this seldom happened. She was unbudgeable in her opinions, but she had a good brain and was very cultivated.'

Carrying on the tradition of the previous tour, all birthdays and holidays were fêted in royal style. Says Elizabeth Frank:

'She always wanted the parties that she gave to be quite different from anything else. I went ahead in Brisbane when they were in Sydney and when I was there she rang up and said, "For the Christmas party, darling, I want you to get a boat. I'll put all the company on a boat and we will have a lovely picnic."

'I said, "A boat? What boat?"

'She said, "Well, just a boat. You can get one. After all you are very competent so you can get a boat."

'I said, "All right then I'll get a boat." And then I asked

around and by incredible luck there was an old show boat in the Brisbane river and I knew that she was prepared to pay quite a lot of money for it. We hired the show boat and she told me what to order for food and drink and everything else. I was already in Perth by the time they had the party. The fact that it was terribly hot and full of mosquitoes did not worry her at all. The members of the company nearly went out of their minds, but it was a lovely idea for her. It had to be something way out, very special.

'On her birthday she was invited to a party by one of the boys' Australian parents and the company had worked for about six weeks to put on a version of *This is Your Life*. They took immense trouble to produce it in incidents that could never possibly have happened to her. For instance, she was born in a slum, became a child acrobat and dancer at the age of six, and then she went to South America in the white slave traffic, that sort of thing. But it was very witty and very amusing and was written by a man in the company called Frank Middlemass. She didn't know that this was going to happen. She arrived and everybody was having drinks and suddenly they turned the lights out and everybody went "Ooooh".

'The lights went on again and one of the actors came forward with a book and said, "Miss Leigh, this is your life." She looked panic-stricken, because she thought they were going to "send her up" or say something embarrassing. And then this started and it was marvellous. It lasted an hour and she was beside herside herself with laughter and also was enormously touched that these people had taken all this trouble to do this for her. She was overcome with it.

'Vivien Leigh *could* be bitchy to girls or boys in the company that she didn't like.

'On the other hand, twenty-one-year-old Caroline

Pertwee, who was her understudy and gave a couple of very good performances when she was off sick on two occasions, had the greatest co-operation. Flowers were sent to her and she received praise. There was another girl whom she was hideous to, through no fault of the girl.'

In the theatre world, her use of the expletive was legendary. She had an idiosyncratic talent in being able to decline her favourite, four-letter verb with alacrity. She used it so frequently that she robbed it of its punch and reduced it almost to a household word, although in certain circumstances she even gave it style.

When Vivien Leigh stood on the draughty, bare stage of the Opera House in Wellington, New Zealand, in 1962 and sang 'I'll be loving you – always' in that low, sultry voice to a darkened empty auditorium, theatrical history was in the making.

For this was the turning point in her indecision as to whether she was good enough to do the musical comedy *Tovarich* on Broadway. In her unsentimental, practical way, Vivien wanted to reassure herself that her voice was strong enough to carry into a theatre. Up till now her efforts had been restricted to round-the-piano efforts at private parties.

Robin Douglas-Home, who used to play the piano at all the smart London parties, recalls her singing at actress Adrienne Allen's show-business marathons at her Hampstead house:

'She would stand by the piano withdrawn from the rest of the party and sing to herself in a husky, intimate, almost wistful voice. She seemed to know all the words of every popular song from 1930 onwards. It was absolutely incredible.'

But now it was completely different and her one-man audience was American producer Abel Farbman. He had flown from New York to New Zealand, where Vivien was travelling with the Old Vic, because he was convinced that no one but she could do justice to the part of the Grand Duchess Tatiana Petronna. Letters and cables to the star had not produced any real progress so he flew to her with the musical score. They had intense, practical talks in Vivien Leigh's hotel suite, but even Farbman's enthusiasm could not sway her. She had to prove to herself that a musical was right for her. To begin with, it was a very strenuous rôle and required her not only to sing but to dance and although all her life, in the normal course of being an actress, she had voice production and singing lessons, she was doubtful whether her voice could carry into an auditorium. She asked for time to consider the whole thing over and Farbman flew back to New York.

One of Vivien Leigh's strongest assets as an actress was her ruthless honesty in knowing exactly her own capabilities and also her ability to judge what was right for her.

Tovarich was originally written as a non-musical play in 1933 when it ran for over eight hundred performances in Paris. The English production in 1935 ran for a year and a day with Eugenie Leontovich and Sir Cedric Hardwicke in the leading rôles. The following year, Claudette Colbert and Charles Boyer starred in an enchanting film, but it was Abel Farbman and Sylvia Harris who were the first to see its possibilities as a musical. Lee Pockriss and lyric writer Anne Crosswell were engaged to write the musical score.

When the Old Vic Company arrived in Mexico City from New Zealand, Mr Farbman flew down again to court Vivien. This time he had a recorded score with him. He played it over and over again to her and left it with her.

She, in turn, promised to let him know her answer in two weeks' time.

To the day, when she was in Buenos Aires, she agreed to sign the contract; 'I've always had a secret longing to do a musical,' she said. 'Everyone always looks as if she was having such fun.'

On arrival back in England from the tour, Vivien Leigh contacted French actor Jean-Pierre Aumont, who had been a friend for over twenty years, and whom Farbman wanted to co-star in *Tovarich*. He had served with the Free French Forces and often stayed with the Oliviers at Notley Abbey.

Jean-Pierre Aumont recalls: 'When the idea of a musical came up neither Vivien nor I had ever done one before. I went over from Paris to Tickeridge Mill and we listened together to the record of the music. That settled it and we decided we'd have a shot at it.'

Before leaving London, Vivien Leigh took a few lessons in singing.

Lee Pockriss, who wrote the songs, described Vivien as having 'goggle appeal'. As he said, 'She is a great lady. No temperament, utterly professional and quite magnificent artist. She came to me to be coached in singing and she was as nervous about singing as I was of teaching her. But everything was fine. She'd start at 10 am and carry on till she nearly dropped. Teaching her to sing was easy. She has a very sweet, rather low voice with an exceptional grasp of metre. When she did something good I'd cry out, "Atta-girl", and she'd burst into laughter and looked pleased like a small schoolgirl.'

Vivien had this to say while rehearsing: 'I won't argue with anyone that I'm not the greatest singer who ever trod the stage, but no one can say that I am not trying. I'm getting better all the time.' Her singing voice, like a Dietrich in miniature, was barely adequate, but she used the technique perfected by Rex Harrison in *My Fair Lady* of speaking the words rather than singing them.

Tovarich opened in Philadelphia and beat all records before moving to Boston. When Vivien did a spirited Charleston, the audience nearly went mad with delight. It stopped the show every night.

Says Jean-Pierre Aumont: 'For the next four weeks we found ourselves going completely mad. Every day some change or another was introduced into the show. At this time there was a change of producers as well – changes in the songs, changes in the dialogue, changes in the stage directions. Sometimes we would rehearse one text in the afternoon and have to play a different one that night. By the time we opened the following March in New York, Vivien was thoroughly exhausted.'

Jean-Pierre Aumont rented a summerhouse at Manhasset and most days Vivien went out there and they would all picnic on the grass. It was the only relaxation they had.

'It was a terribly tiring rôle for her. She had a great number of costume changes and, of course, there was the fact that she had never done a musical before. You couldn't call Vivien a great singer and dancer but she had such elegance and grace that people were enchanted by her. She had a kind of magic. As soon as she appeared on stage, people fell under her charm. Then, of course, she was more than an actress, she was a legend – Lady Olivier, Shakespearean actress, star of *Gone With the Wind* and *Streetcar*. There was something at once comic and ravishing about seeing this fabulous woman play a soubrette in a white apron and suddenly break into a song and dance routine.'

The staid *Philadelphia Inquirer* wrote, 'In her humour, dignity and quiet comedy, Miss Vivien Leigh is warming and commanding. As a vocalist she is less persuasive.'

In New York where *Tovarich* opened on 18th March, a

221

protracted newspaper strike kept the theatre critics silent, but as Walter Kerr of the *New York Herald Tribune* later said, 'Vivien Leigh is one of the crown jewels. She and Jean-Pierre Aumont cast a personal glow over a handsome, friendly and affectionate show'. John Chapman, drama critic of the *New York Daily News* wrote: 'Vivien Leigh is incredibly beautiful, incredibly graceful and incredibly charming. She would make any musical in which she appeared distinguished, but *Tovarich* is a distinguished musical in its own right.' William Glover of the Associated Press raved, 'Miss Vivien Leigh is a nifty cutie pie in her first work out in the song and dance stage.' After the opening night there was a brilliant supper party at which both the Duchess of Buccleuch and Alan Pryce Jones were present. Recalling this night Pryce Jones says: 'I remember clearly how marvellous Vivien Leigh was, how supple and incredibly young. She had got back her old form and was passed from shoulder to shoulder by the chorus as though she was eighteen again.'

Vivien Leigh won the 1963 Tony Award on Broadway which is show business's equivalent to an Oscar for her performance in *Tovarich*.

The heat in New York was oppressive and as Vivien said, 'I spent hours each day bathed in perspiration.' She began getting overtired and suffering from terrible headaches. Finally during a scene where she had to portray great exasperation and jealousy, she forgot her lines and walked off the stage. The rest of the cast covered for her until she reappeared. According to *Paris Match* she suddenly began beating Jean-Pierre Aumont and could not stop. But he rejects this and says the incident was grossly exaggerated.

After the show had been playing ten months at the Broadway Theatre, Vivien's New York doctors advised her to go back to London and consult her own physician.

Again in a state of complete exhaustion she was carried aboard the air liner under sedation and her face covered with a piece of white gauze. She was completely screened off from the other passengers.

Four days later, after her dramatic flight back, writer David Lewin called to see her. She greeted him at the door looking absolutely refreshed and well, wearing a rich blue velvet cat suit.

'I suppose it is silly for me at my age,' she said, 'to go jumping up and down doing the Charleston with my heart pounding and on matinée days bathed in sweat for six hours at a time. But I did it and I loved it. I knew I would be ill, but I was not given a holiday because the show had to go on. And then it happened.

'After I played in Tripoli in the war when the temperature was 120 degrees I thought I'd never mind the heat again. But in New York the humidity was worse. What I have learned from *Tovarich* is patience. I have a lot of patience now.'

The show moved to the Wintergarden, and Eva Gabor took over her rôle.

'I think Vivien acquired a taste for musical comedies and might have gone on with them if things had been different,' says Jean-Pierre Aumont. 'She liked the family atmosphere you get with an enormous cast and people getting married and having babies during the run. She always had a prodigious memory for people and faces, and took a tremendous interest in the lives of her acquaintances. Some years before *Tovarich* I was on a holiday with her in Tourraine. Suddenly in a small village she stopped the postman in the street and asked him how he was and whether his daughter Henriette was married yet. She had been there two years before and made friends with all the local people. It was the same wherever we went.

'Vivien was an irresistible personality. She was inclined to fits of temperament but she was the most loyal of friends. She remained very devoted to Laurence Olivier, his photograph was always in her dressing room. She often talked about him to me but I do not think she ever revealed to anybody what she felt in the depths of her heart.

'I shall never forget my last meeting with her. My wife and I had a cabaret engagement at the Persian Room in New York. And one night, suddenly, there was Vivien. I sang my way round the room until I reached her table and embraced her.

' "Come and sing *Tovarich* with me," she said. I protested that the band hadn't got the music.

' "Never mind, come on," she said. I said I had forgotten the words.

' "Never mind, never mind."

'We got up and, without any accompaniment, began to sing the songs from *Tovarich*. The audience in the Persian Room went mad.

'That night we had supper together until five in the morning. Vivien never wanted to go to bed early. The next morning she left for London. Six months later she was dead.'

The Last Act

FAN LOVE IS a very mystical and tender experience. To Vivien Leigh's fans she was a goddess made of flesh and blood. She was not the unattainable like Garbo to be worshipped from the stalls. Instead she was a very real person and a woman of infinite kindness. They, the fans, were friends to be remembered whenever she could fit in time in her busy life.

She had the engaging and frugal habit of collecting postcards and hotel stationery on her travels and using them at a later date, even in a different country. Her envelopes often bore the name of a New York hotel but the fun was finding out that the letter came from New Zealand. This added spice to her correspondence.

Typical of Vivien's meticulous care for her fans is the fact that just three weeks before she died, in July 1967, she wrote from her bed to Joyce Huddart of London on a card printed in L'Alibigeois. The writing was less disciplined than usual and was obviously written under some strain.

June 15

My dear Joyce,
Thank you for your very sweet letter. I am so thankful the play has only been postponed not cancelled that it makes this stupid rest easier.

Fond wishes
Vivien Leigh

She was referring to the Albee play *A Delicate Balance*

in which she was to star with Sir Michael Redgrave in August. When Joyce's mother died, in the various cards Vivien sent her, she always wrote comforting words.

'It is just the way she remembered the small things that made her so marvellous,' Marguerita Malyon said, near to tears.

Many of the girls became friends through meeting each other at the stage door, a fact Vivien Leigh did not necessarily know. They always showed each other their cards or letters but in all the dozens there was never one the same.

'We always knew when Miss Leigh had not written a card which did not happen very often. It was not as warm and not the kind of words that she would use.'

Whenever Vivien Leigh was in London, Joyce Huddart, who works in an office, sent her flowers every week.

'I just loved to do it and there was no other reason. I used to try and get white flowers or sweet-smelling ones which I knew she liked. She didn't acknowledge every bouquet but then I would never have expected her to – she led a very busy life.'

Though it was several months after Vivien Leigh's death Marguerita Malyon still could not believe that she would not see Vivien Leigh again.

'I went to the memorial service and cried all the way through. I cannot really believe it now. She was such a wonderful person and we saw a side of her that no one else would have. I only wish more people had known what she was really like. Whatever we did for her it was a two-way traffic.'

Finding gifts for Vivien Leigh – the woman with everything – was always a challenge to her fans. In sending her a gift perhaps they gained even more pleasure than Vivien Leigh.

'We tried to find out everything about her life and looked for any tiny clue that would help us. But as Miss Leigh gave relatively few personal interviews it was sometimes difficult. We were always looking for things that would give her pleasure as well as being practical.'

For Christmas one year Marguerita found two packs of miniature patience cards which Vivien Leigh always took with her when she travelled.

'We read that she liked to play patience and when I saw them I knew that they might be useful.'

A small closing ashtray for her handbag (Vivien Leigh was a consistent smoker) and a telephone index book were other presents they found. One of the last gifts that Joyce Huddart sent before the Oliviers separated was a miniature of Laurence Olivier in the costume of the first *Hamlet*.

'It was a very lovely miniature and Miss Leigh said that she would always treasure it,' Joyce now relates sadly.

For her fans the split up in the Olivier marriage was a very real and personal tragedy. In some cases they had been first the fans of Laurence Olivier and then embraced Vivien Leigh. In other cases it had often worked in reverse.

When the news of the final separation was reported in 1959 the fans were completely shattered.

How could two people who had given each other so much not find a way out of their present difficulties. They met to discuss the situation and try to explain to each other the cause of it all.

Having no direct contact with Vivien Leigh about it they bought every newspaper, every magazine that might be able to throw any light on the event. Their only wish was to protect her from the loneliness of divorce.

'I used to be a fan of Sir Laurence's but not now,' another girl explained. 'Laurence Olivier and Vivien Leigh were like royalty and this marriage should never have been broken. They belonged together.'

After the news of the separation the fans vowed even more love and loyalty to Vivien Leigh.

'We used to go to the stage door as often as possible and though we never mentioned the fact of the divorce we knew that she was grateful that we admired her and wanted to know her even more than before. I have seen her face showing great strain and distress and looking very sad, but she seemed to change after the divorce and become even more wonderful and interested in our lives.'

Vivien Leigh's fans were not invited to her home and hardly ever into her theatre dressing room. Snatched conversations were exchanged at the stage door usually after a show. But this was enough. They didn't expect more. Apart from these encounters and her letters Vivien Leigh was also practical towards her fans. If they could not get tickets for the new show because of heavy bookings, she invariably managed to send them some. Once when she was rehearsing at the theatre she arranged that two of the girls were able to attend several rehearsals despite the fact that it was well known that she disliked outsiders present during these hours.

For five years after her divorce Vivien Leigh did not send her fans any Christmas cards. Then suddenly, Christmas 1965, they all received an Oxfam card and Christmas 1966 a photo of her newest home, Tickeridge Mill.

Though willing to discuss Vivien Leigh's acting ability, the strange thing is that this was not the moving factor in her fans' admiration. Some of them were even critical and thought that she was in plays that did not suit her.

'Of course she was a great actress and always looked so beautiful but this is not what made us like her. It is difficult to explain,' said Marguerita Malyon.

Perhaps the explanation lies in the fact that Vivien Leigh

had always behaved and looked the part of the star that they believed her to be. She had never let them down by being ungracious or unglamorous. She inspired in them the same devotion that she received from her friends because few people could resist her.

When Vivien Leigh made her second march through London to save the St James's Theatre her fans were there to support her. They felt that by just being there they were giving some support to the small figure striding out there in front whom they admired. And when the memorial service was held after Vivien Leigh's death, along with all the famous from London's theatre land were the faithful sprinkling of fans. Somehow they had all managed to get time off from their various jobs to say their own goodbye.

To each of her fans there can never be anyone else like Vivien Leigh. This magnolia beauty had brought a touch of magic to their lives. No one can possibly take her place.

'She was so wonderful,' is their own epitaph.

In latter years Vivien Leigh was preoccupied with the tragedy of ageing beauty. Her last two films, *The Roman Spring of Mrs Stone* (1961) and *Ship of Fools* (1965), as well as the last stage play, *La Contessa* (1965), all dealt with this theme. It was as though she felt that it was something that every beauty has to face in reality and she would do it publicly before it became necessary in private. Most of the films she made after the war had tragic endings.

'Glamour has nothing to do with age. I do not consider that a woman in her forties is old. Dame Sybil Thorndike is well over seventy' [she was then seventy-nine] 'and she is about the youngest person I've ever met in vitality,' she said.

'I do not worry about my looks because beauty is not a thing of age but of spirit. Look at Lady Diana Cooper or

Dame Edith Evans, two of the most beautiful women I know.'

But despite this it took Hollywood director Stanley Kramer a trip to England and many transatlantic telephone calls to persuade her to play the part of Mary Treadwell, the forty-six-year-old Virginian in *Ship of Fools*. The rest of the cast, including two other Academy award winners – Simone Signoret and José Ferrer – had been chosen long before Vivien Leigh would finally agree. Her signature on the contract reads 'Vivien Leigh Olivier'. In describing the part later, Vivien said, 'I think that what the actor or actress can contribute to society is to reveal character, make people understand other people better – all kinds of people.

'In *Ship of Fools* I'm Mary Treadwell. She's escaping from life whenever she possibly can. She's a romantic at heart who cannot reconcile her present life with the life she used to live. She's very much alone, aloof and outwardly composed but with an underlying passion.

'I don't think I've ever played a part like it before.' And she seldom played one as well.

Vivien Leigh's return in April 1964 to Hollywood was momentous. The film colony treated the whole thing as nothing short of a royal visit.

Even such sophisticates as Katherine Hepburn, a friend of many years, and director George Cukor of *Gone With the Wind*, were caught up in the fervour. It is a reflection of Vivien Leigh's magic that she inspired people to give of their very best for her – just as she did for them. She telephoned George Cukor from London and asked if he would find her a house in Hollywood. She never liked to stay in hotels if she could avoid it.

'This was a big responsibility,' says Cukor, 'so I called in Kate Hepburn. She's marvellous at that sort of thing. We climbed in and out of several houses before we found the right one as we took our responsibilities very seriously.'

They settled on a small green two-storey house in Beverly Hills.

'We thought now we can't have anything that isn't right for Vivien, so we asked various friends to lend things. Rex Evans lent her pictures and Kate and I put some bits and pieces around. Although it was a very nice house we tried to make it the way Vivien would like it. We even hired a cook and arranged the first meal.

'When we came back from meeting her at the airport there was this lovely moment of suspense as Kate and I tasted everything and looked at each other. It was perfect. Vivien simply adored the house and despite the fact that Mrs Evans had filled it with flowers she went around and bought more and more flowers and plants until we had to stop her. Then she went and moved everything round until it was just how she wanted it.

'After that first meal Vivien asked who did this and who did that. She ticked it all off and thanked everyone who had done anything for her. I have never known anyone so appreciative if anything was done for her. She was fundamentally kind. To be constantly kind and have constant good manners that is a very educated soul.'

On the set of *Ship of Fools* there was amused apprehension as to how Vivien Leigh and Simone Signoret, who was to co-star, would get on together. It was hard to imagine such wildly different and strong-willed women – the highly professional, self-contained Vivien who played everything through her intellect, and the volatile and emotional Simone, the instinctive actress over-spilling with heart.

Director Stanley Kramer did his part. Both stars were given identical living allowances of four dollar figures a week. Both had equally lavish dressing rooms and matching chauffeur-driven limousines. Vivien was to be given first billing in English-speaking countries and Simone top elsewhere.

As was her habit, Vivien did not disclose her salary, but Simone said she was paid £50,000, so presumably Vivien received as much if not more.

George Cukor, a close friend of both actresses, was brought in to make the initial informal introductions. It was important for everyone that they get off in the right way. He invited them both to dinner at his house in Beverly Hills.

'They didn't like each other on sight,' says Cukor.

'Simone, who has to play a pill-addicted countess in the film, would say something about that she never took pills. "I over-do everything. If I took pills I would be a drug addict in a week."

'Vivien turned round rather coolly and said, "I love pills. I am constantly taking them."

'They just went on all night contradicting each other. It was terribly funny. The next day they called up and they were both awfully nice, sincere, decent women. They turned out to be great friends.

'Vivien was full of prejudices but she was not petty. She had no bitchery in her. She realised that Simone was a good-hearted person and a very fine actress.'

When John Gielgud arrived to make *The Loved One* he became Vivien's house guest, as well as Jack Merivale. Hollywood hostesses vied with each other to fête her but she begged off big parties. Instead every Sunday she filled her house with roses and friends. Once or twice she went to night clubs, escorted by Merivale, where she loved to dance. Tipped off by the reservations clerk, the musicians would greet her with the theme music from *Gone With the Wind* and the other guests noticing her would all rise to clap. It was like old times and Vivien bloomed to the celebrity treatment. Gielgud had promised Vivien Leigh to show her Disneyland and this became one of the mad, wonderful nights of her stay.

At the neighbouring restaurant at Columbia Studios The Naples, where the film people lunch, a waitress remembers:

'She ate here every day, and a nicer person it's never been my privilege to wait on. So unassuming you'd think she was nobody. Just lovely.'

Celebrities often make a point of being courteous to waitresses but Tennessee Williams explains Vivian succinctly:

'She had an instinct for saying and doing just the right thing to put you at your ease – even when you knew you were making a fool of yourself.'

With nine separate plots spinning at once in *Ship of Fools*, few of Vivien Leigh's twenty-three fellow artists had scenes with her. When Oskar Werner, the reigning Hamlet of the German-speaking stage, who played Dr Schumann in the film, met Abby Mann, the script writer, he greeted him with:

'By the way, I have no scenes with Miss Leigh. I want you to write some in for me.'

Abby Mann looked at him through his brash, black lenses and replied: 'Are you kidding? You're only the sixth actor who's asked me.'

The set was always packed with actors and actresses when Vivien was working. Even outside players from other studios pleaded to be allowed to enter into Kramer's kingdom.

It was not only that watching Vivien at work was to see a professional's pro but she brought back to the studios an aura of glamour and excitement that had been missing since the thirties and everyone was quick to appreciate it.

Vivien Leigh gave few interviews and when she did found them tiresome and banal and the interviewers found her dull and conventional. For instance, when a television interviewer presented her to his audience as 'a living legend – Scarlett O'Hara', he had not reckoned on Vivien's come-back.

'Good heavens,' she said, 'I've played scores of rôles since that one and if my luck holds out I'll play scores more. Let's talk about Mary Treadwell, for instance.'

To one famous columnist her answers were drearily safe:

'I do enjoy working in Hollywood. It's so wonderfully efficient. Everybody seems so deeply interested in what they're doing, and I've always found that people have been tremendously helpful and considerate. I've loved every time I've worked here.'

'The statements from Buckingham Palace are not exactly titillating either,' commented the reporter.

One of the most tender moments of the three months making the film was the day white-haired, ageing Spencer Tracy went out to the studio to see Vivien on set. They greeted each other with a big hug and kiss and there was scarcely a dry eye around. It was Spencer Tracy who had presented her with the Oscar she won in *Gone With the Wind*.

In the Movieland Wax Museum she heard that just as she was in Madame Tussaud's in London she was there as Scarlett, along with Clark Gable as Rhett Butler and Hattie McDaniel as Mammy. But she would not go near the place:

'It makes me so sad to think of that picture here in Hollywood now,' she said. 'So many of its people are dead – Clark, Leslie [Howard], Walter [Connolly], dear Hattie, Victor [Fleming, the director] and even Margaret Mitchell . . . the last time I saw the film I wept all the way through it.'

Many film writers predicted that Vivien in the part of the

self-centred, coy, caustic, withered Mary Treadwell in *Ship of Fools* would win yet another Oscar. She did not but she was awarded the title of best foreign actress of that year by the French Film Academy.

There is one scene that every young actress should be shown as an example of the technique of film acting at its professional peak. Mary Treadwell – who boasted of her dead husband: 'I made life hell for him' – is alone in her cabin. She had just been brutally told by a man: 'You are a forty-six-year-old woman and you'll end up sitting in night clubs with a paid gigolo.' She returns to her cabin and the scene is in horrifying close-up. Her face is violent, the eyes wild and searching, nostrils flared.

She savagely daubs her face with the make-up of a younger woman and cries.

'You are not young, Mrs Treadwell. You have not been young for years. But behind those old eyes you hide a sixteen-year-old heart. Poor fool. Is that what men really find attractive?'

The scene is brutal, truthful and magnificent. Vivien Leigh stretched out and reached her height.

All the way through the film, Vivien kept a copy of Katherine Anne Porter's novel in her dressing room; just as she had done with *Gone With the Wind*.

'I think it's important to know the book thoroughly and Mr Kramer doesn't seem to mind,' she said. 'He knew it backwards himself. But I remember David Selznick did mind. He'd come into my dressing room and say: "Put that damn book away."

'I try to assimilate the author's interpretation and stick to it,' she explained. 'What else is there to stick to? That's what we're indebted to, after all. The first duty of the actor is to be true to what the author intended.'

The critics were unanimous in their praise of Vivien

Leigh. As Ernest Betts wrote: 'Though Vivien's big scene is sheer melodrama, she manages to convey by acting ability of a high order the tragedy of a woman with nothing to live for.'

When a girl friend of Vivien Leigh saw the film she remarked to her that she found it incredible that such a beautiful and rich woman as Mary Treadwell could get into such a state of insecurity.

'My darling, that is the one thing true about that film. I know,' replied Vivien.

It is ironical and sad that Vivien Leigh, twice Academy Award winner, Broadway Tony Award winner and French Academy winner as best foreign actress of 1964, should give the last theatre performance of her life in a play that was a failure at the Opera House, Manchester, on 29th April 1965.

Just back from a holiday in Katmandu and after six years' absence from the English stage, during which time she had been mainly acting abroad, Vivien Leigh planned a comeback with *La Contessa*, a play based on the novel *Film of Memory* by French author Maurice Druon. It was a fascinating story based on the life of the eccentric Italian Marquesa Casati, who had died only nine years before.

Born to immense wealth and married into riches, the Marquesa scrambled through a couple of fortunes with the insouciance of an orphanage child. She was magnificently dotty with her three palazzios (Venice, Rome and Florence), a private zoo which she shuttled along wherever she travelled and two pet panthers which she dragged reluctantly through the streets of Paris.

This magnificent old trout, who claimed to be the mistress of the Kaiser and a friend of Axel Munthe and d'Annunzio, was seventy-seven years of age when she died.

Desiccated, raddled and utterly terrifying, she had dyed

her hair bright orange and rimmed her eyes with black tape. The play takes place in a shabby Rome hotel where she sits in a holocaust unable to disassociate the fabulous past with the pathetic commonplace present.

It was a terrifying rôle suited to actresses of such nobility and splendour of voice as Dame Margaret Rutherford and Dame Edith Evans. But aged fifty-one and looking still ravishingly pretty, Vivien Leigh was too lightweight for the part.

'I read *La Contessa* in 1962 and ever since I have wanted to play it. It is a composite of many women,' she said.

Robert Helpmann, long friend of the Oliviers, was asked by H M Tennent Ltd to direct and Vivien Leigh agreed to stay in the play for six months and no longer.

'It always strikes me as something curious that actors are supposed to do the same thing night after night – dancers don't, cricketers don't, painters don't. Why should actors?' she explained. In fact few actors and actresses like a run lasting longer than six months.

Talking on the opening night to John Stevenson of the Manchester *Daily Mail*, Vivien Leigh said:

'It's not that I haven't wanted to appear in England, and I have been offered several good parts. But my commitments have taken me abroad and only now have I been able to return.

'I read this play three years ago. I don't know whether it will succeed or whether it will flop. I feel excitement and terror – and am very anxious to try it. The part of the old countess is something entirely new for me. I've never played a woman of this age before – but age is a question of how you feel. And although this woman is seventy-seven, she's a very interesting and exciting person, which is all that matters.'

It was an ambitious production involving fourteen

scene changes. What went wrong was that instead of seeing a devastating old frump, the audience were greeted by Vivien Leigh as beautiful as ever, in a marmalade wig with her eye make-up smudged. She could not bear to look ravaged and yet it was ludicrous to look so attractive. It made nonsense of the whole plot. This was a vehicle for someone meant to frighten you, not like an ingenue who had raided the attic trunks.

The play was received by a mainly critical press and the audiences were described as 'fair'.

As *The Sun* said: 'On stage, Miss Leigh, at fifty-one, grasps the essence of this woman's eccentricity, she sways and trembles with the frailty of old age. But her voice comes over as clear and strong as ever.'

'Vivien Leigh, even under heavy make-up, does not look to be seventy-plus. She moves too beautifully and speaks appallingly hackneyed lines with too much conviction for that,' wrote one reviewer. Another dismissed it with: 'It is by no means easy to find a good word for this play.'

There were rumours that the play was being taken off.

Before going on stage at Liverpool, Vivien Leigh said: 'I have not been told what is happening. I think my part is a good one, but whether it was the right part for me to take I just don't know. If I knew that kind of thing I would be a very rich woman.

'The trouble is that theatre-goers don't want to see me playing a finished old woman. They want to see me as a glamour symbol. They hate my appearance so they don't like the play. If the structure was different and throughout the play I appeared in a flashback middle sequence as the beauty I was supposed to have been, I think we would have had a success.'

A statement from the management next day put an end

to any hopes for the West End. John Stevenson, who spoke to her just after she had heard the depressing news (the play had intended even going on to Broadway), says:

'At the time it was impossible not to help feeling admiration for her. She was terribly upset about the killing of the show and yet she trouped away bravely to the bitter end. As she said to me:

' "She's old and pathetic and that's why it seemed to me that playing this part would build a bridge to parts where I don't have to be a beautiful woman whatever else I am. I thought it would make me acceptable as an actress who didn't have to be cast in that way any more. It's all gone hopelessly wrong, of course, but whether it's the play's fault, or mine, or the audiences', I don't know."

'The last two weeks must have been very unhappy ones for Vivien. The play had nowhere to go. There was nothing to look forward to and not much point left in the entire exercise. But at every performance, in a very demanding part, Vivien gave everyone full value. She never coasted through a single performance.'

Vivien Leigh's professional integrity made up for any acting shortcomings she may have had. She simply never let her public down.

Curtain

WHY DID VIVIEN LEIGH die? Why in this enlightened medical age should anyone with tuberculosis die alone in their bedroom in their own apartment within taxi distance of one of the great tubercular centres in the world.

The answer is that in fact no one, not even her doctors, realised that the tuberculosis they had first noticed in 1946 had developed into what is commonly called galloping consumption. Tests had been taken some weeks before but the results were not known until she had died.

The test for tuberculosis is quite simple. Guinea pigs are injected with the patient's sputum. If after six weeks the guinea pig has developed tuberculosis it is then known that the disease is again active in the patient.

It was not until the post mortem that the seriousness of her illness was really discovered. Had anyone – and that means her doctors, mother, daughter and close friend of the last seven years, Jack Merivale – thought that her life was in danger she would have been overruled and placed in a hospital fully equipped for any emergencies.

Even Vivien Leigh herself had no idea how ill she was. To her friends who saw her in that last week she always talked about feeling stronger and being allowed to go to her country house in Sussex the following week.

Just before midnight on Friday, 7th July 1967 Vivien Leigh was found dead by Jack Merivale. He had returned from Brighton where he was in a play and on arrival had gone in to the bedroom to see her. Later he went to the kitchen to get something to eat from the refrigerator. He heard a noise and rushed back to the bedroom to find that she had fallen as if she had been trying to get out of bed.

This exhausted, fragile little body had been unable to fight to live any longer. It seems ironic that one of the world's great beauties who spent a lifetime surrounding herself with people should be alone when she died.

Vivien had always loved her rose-filled bedroom which she had transformed into a bower. The walls were entirely hung with white chintz splashed with bright pink old-fashioned roses.

Over the large bed flowed canopied curtains of the same chintz, with filmy linings of white and pale pink nylon. Her favourite pictures hung on silk cords against the folds of chintz on the walls – the small Berthe Moreset, a sketch by Augustus John, a tiny Cellini drawing and a vase of roses which Sir Winston Churchill had painted specially for her.

The bathroom leading off her bedroom was rose-filled – wall paper, bath surround and bath towels. There were flowers everywhere, carnations and pink roses. Even when she was ill Vivien insisted on getting up each day for an hour to arrange her own flowers. On the small table was a pile of the latest books and on the wall photographs of the three men she admired – Sir Winston Churchill, Bernard Baruch the American financier and of course Laurence Olivier.

It was theatre – sheer theatre – a setting for Titania, Juliet or Ophelia. And those who loved Vivien Leigh were thankful. She would have wanted it this way, surrounded by her own feminine and personal world.

All the last week Vivien filled her life with people. The day before she died she was rehearsing her part with Michael Redgrave in the Edward Albee play *A Delicate Balance* scheduled to open in August. She was convinced that she would be well enough for the opening night and that the play would not have to be postponed again.

On the days when she felt well enough her vitality bubbled through. She was gay, funny and bewitching. At other times she looked pale and wan and would repeat:

'I am tired, so very tired. If only I could have a lovely long sleep and wake up fresh again.'

Sir Michael tells of when she appeared exhausted and transparently tired:

'It was as if she could hardly get the words out. It was like a child trying to say the lines we were rehearsing. Then we would have to stop.'

Writer Robin Douglas-Home, who had worshipped her since he was a schoolboy of fifteen, called to see her a few days before she died. He had gone to see her to discuss a series of articles he intended to write about her.

'I was frankly shocked by the face that smiled to greet me from the pillows. The exquisite pert nose, the wonderfully round eyes, the swan's neck and grandeur of features – they were all there just as they had been when I had last seen her at a Mayfair lunch a few weeks ago.

'But the colour had left her cheeks, her lips were dulled, the lustre of her eyes were dimmed and her skin lifeless.

' "I'm over the worst part," she said definitely and defiantly. "Only a few more days in bed here, then the doctors say I can go and convalesce in my house in Sussex."

'But I had only to look into that parchment face to know that this could not really be so. I knew, and I had to struggle to prevent myself from showing that I knew, that this outstandingly beautiful woman had already surrendered to the cold grasp of death.

'But there was no trace of surrender in her mood or in her demeanour. Her throaty laughter, crackling with all her old appeal, rang out again and again.'

Actor Emlyn Williams, and his wife, Molly, who knew Vivien Leigh for thirty years, saw her the day before she died.

'She looked wonderful in bed. She wore no make-up and had just had her hair cut a new style. She looked like a sweet little girl. We loved her so and miss her terribly.'

That same evening she had a private film show in her bedroom. Stanley Hall, who had been making wigs for Vivien Leigh for over thirty years, and was a close friend and neighbour in Sussex, took along film equipment to amuse her.

Friends who knew that she would be alone in the evenings during the week while Merivale was in Brighton took it in turn to visit her so that she would not be lonely.

She lay back in bed 'under sedation but her usual scintillating self' while he showed her two films – *Rembrandt's Paintings* and another called *Shakespeare Wallah* which was about a touring company in India. 'We laughed and talked about exchanging plants for our gardens, the grandchildren and theatre news, as we always did.'

Although the plain medical facts of Vivien Leigh's death was tuberculosis, her friends still tend to romanticise.

'Everything finished for her the day Laurence Olivier left. She had never accepted the divorce,' Sir Michael Redgrave, who had known her for thirty years, recalls.

Another friend: 'She had never got over her serious error of judgment in thinking that Larry would never leave her. She was so sensitive in her appraisal of people generally, but here she had failed. And this hurt her deeply. She did not seem to want to go on living.'

Her neighbour and friend for many years, Lady Audley (Sarah Churchill) says wistfully: 'She folded her wings and turned her face to the wall.'

'She died of a broken heart,' is how another friend put it bluntly.

Each marriage has its heart, its core, which can only possibly be felt and understood by the two people concerned.

In the case of Vivien Leigh and Laurence Olivier theirs was a very lasting tie. Their concern for each other was touching. They saw each other regularly and spoke by phone.

'Larry darling, are you taking care of yourself and not getting too tired? . . .'

'Puss, do listen to what the doctors say. . . .'

Although she always said that she intended going on acting until she was eighty years old, and never gave death a thought, Vivien Leigh had in fact left her affairs in immaculate order.

Her wish for her eyes to be used for corneal grafting was unable to be carried out due to the tuberculosis. She knew about this when making her will but she wanted the request put in in the hope that it would encourage others to give their eyes.

For this same reason, too, no insurance company would cover Vivien Leigh during any of her productions – a hazard which had to be considered by any company employing her.

Vivien Leigh left an estate valued at £252,681 gross, before duty of £41,429, most of which went to her daughter Suzanne, Mrs Robin Farrington. A private letter which she left to her executors to be opened on her death gave instructions for the disposal of the £12,000 worth of pictures, jewellery and furniture that she left among her close friends.

'I don't know whether in fact I am a wealthy woman. I have no idea of the amount of money I have,' she used to say. But in fact although she appeared vague she was a shrewd investor, and left considerably more money than her friends expected.

Apart from her association with Laurence Olivier Productions, she had also formed her own company called Vivien Leigh Productions. This company had invested in such West End successes as *Roar of a Dove*, *Taste of Honey*, *The Hostage*, *Loot* and *Make Me An Offer*.

A family Requiem Mass for Vivien Leigh was held in the Roman Catholic Church of St Mary's, Cadogan Street, London on 12th July 1967, at ten o'clock. The Mass was said by Canon Longstaff and the coffin was graced by her favourite white roses picked from her garden at Tickeridge Mill in Sussex. There was just her immediate family present. Sir Laurence Olivier did not attend but his son Tarquin did.

After the service, according to her own instructions, she was cremated at the Golders Green Crematorium.

The evening after she died, on 8 July, London's theatre-land paid its own special tribute to this glittering star. All over the West End between 10 pm and 11 pm the theatre lights dimmed in tribute to her courage as a woman and to her professionalism as an actress.

Outside were the lifeless lights and inside the performances went on – just as Vivien herself would have wished. It was a touching gesture to the woman who had said:

'Being a film star – just a film star is such a false life, living for false values. Actresses go on for a long time and there are always marvellous parts to play. I don't ever want to retire – I want to act until I am ninety.'

On 15th August, five weeks after her death, the actors and actresses of London gathered at eleven o'clock at the Royal Parish Church of St Martin's-in-the-Fields for their own memorial service. It was to this church courtyard, fringing Trafalgar Square, that Vivien had led her supporters after the march through London to protest against the demolition of St James's Theatre.

As they mounted the twenty-seven steps the names were like a roll call of the greatest in the world of the theatre.

Twenty minutes before the service was due to begin the vast church was almost full. They were all there, the hundreds of friends who had mingled with Vivien Leigh in her thirty-two years of acting, each remembering in the comforting shadows of the church his or her own private encounter. For Vivien Leigh's greatest achievement was that she was a woman first and actress second.

There was Dame Peggy Ashcroft and Anna Neagle who were both asked but were unable to play the part of Henrietta in *The Mask of Virtue*, which brought Vivien fame overnight.

Miss Cicely Courtneidge, escorted by her husband, Jack Hulbert, remembered the quicksilver prettiness of the young Vivien who played a schoolgirl in *Things are Looking Up*. Miss Courtneidge was the star and Vivien the eager ingenue.

Robert Cooke's memory must have flashed back to that now historical weekend with Vivien Leigh and Laurence Olivier on the Douglas Fairbanks' yacht off Catalina Island. Together they listened to Chamberlain's declaration of war. For Herbert Wilcox there was the poignant moment of his severe illness in 1965. The first of the flowers to arrive were Vivien's massive, white azalea.

Miss Dorothy Dickson had seen Vivien, a friend from wartime years, just two days before she died when she had confided how she planned to build a playroom for her grandchildren at Tickeridge Mill.

For John Clements, who read the lesson from the Revelation of St John, there were all the giggles they had

246

in the 'all-star concert party' which visited aerodromes and launched the RAF Benevolent Fund.

The soberly-suited man was playwright Terence Rattigan, an especially close colleague. Their private wit together was diamond bright.

Lady Redgrave recalled how she first met Vivien when she came to see her in hospital after Lynn Redgrave was born.

One hour before the service began Sir Laurence Olivier slipped in alone at the back of the church. In the gloom, shorter than his stage image, few people recognised him as he sheltered by a pillar and stood beside an old friend, Ginette Spanier.

Leigh Holman, Vivien's first husband who had loved her from the day he first saw her in 1932, accompanied their daughter, Suzanne, Mrs Robin Farrington, and Vivien's mother, Mrs Gertrude Hartley. Beside them were the two small boys who gravely called this great star 'grandmama'.

Sir John Gielgud, friend of the Oliviers for over thirty years, in vowels of pure gold gave the address:

'One almost felt bitter resentment at the suddenness of her end. So triumphant were her films that she could have earned vast sums by acting only in them. But she was stubborn in her determination to reach the heights in the theatre.'

He referred to her years with Laurence Olivier who stood grave with head bent. Theirs had been one of the most glamorous and decorative marriages of the theatre.

'This marriage was an inspiration to her. Their performances together in plays, not only in this country but all over the world, brought fresh laurels to her crown. She had a truly magical quality.' Saying that even in her later years Vivien never harboured resentment as she saw younger actresses climbing to triumphs he added:

'Let us salute her for all that she gave the world.'

After John Clements had read the lesson, Emlyn Williams quoted from John Donne's *Of the Progresse of the Soule*.

Standing before the altar, Rachel Kempson (Lady Redgrave) made each word glow as she read these prayers by St Francis of Assisi. The works of St Francis were by Vivien Leigh's bedside when she died.

> *Make me an instrument of Your peace*
> *Where there is hatred, let me sow love;*
> *Where there is injury, pardon; where*
> *there is doubt, faith; where there is*
> *despair, hope; where there is darkness,*
> *light; and where there is sadness, joy.*

> *O Divine Master*
> *Grant that I may not so much seek to be*
> *consoled as to console; to be understood*
> *as to understand; to be loved as to love;*
> *For it is only in giving that we receive;*
> *it is in pardoning that we are pardoned; it is*
> *in dying that we are born to eternal life.*

It was immensely dignified and impressive. As the congregation shuffled out into the daylight there was only the snap of a handbag as a handkerchief was extracted.

On the afternoon of the second Sunday in July 1967, the old girls of the Sacred Heart Convent at Roehampton were holding their regular reunion. News of the death of their school colleague Vivien Leigh had filled the morning papers.

Vivien Leigh had not always been a faithful Catholic,

believing that she had found her own philosophy and had come to terms with herself.

'Perhaps people will think of me in the way I have tried to behave towards them. "Use all gently" [from *Hamlet*]. It has a good sound for a simple thought,' she used to say.

The old girls who remembered the bubbling schoolgirl over the years asked for a prayer for her soul. The Reverend Mother Shanley lifted her hands.

'Now let us say the *De Profundis* for Vivian Mary Hartley: *Out of the depth I cry to thee. Oh Lord, hear my voice* . . .'

The whole school wept.

Epilogue

ON THE DAY after the news of Vivien Leigh's death some unknown person from London's 7,880,760 citizens scratched these words on the column outside No 53 Eaton Square where she had lived:

A great actress for ever and ever. We vote you the young at heart and a true beauty

Index

251